We Were Meant for Paradise

Devotions for the journey Home

Lisa Buffaloe

We Were Meant for Paradise

John 15:11 Publications
Copyright 2017 Lisa Buffaloe (Revised July 2023)

Visit the author's website at https://lisabuffaloe.com

ISBN-13: 978-0692938980
ISBN-10: 0692938982

Cover photo and design: Lisa Buffaloe

Printed in the United States of America

To my wonderful Heavenly Father.
Thank You for bringing me into Your family through
the mercy and grace of Your Son, Jesus Christ.
Thank You that one day Your followers
will be with You in paradise.

We Were Meant for Paradise

We were meant for paradise, a place to meet with God where our souls are in tune with our Maker. We were meant for God's fellowship; that's why we long for more and why so many seek a pathway leading to peace and happiness.

God created the heavens and the earth, created a garden, a perfect place -- paradise. Adam and Eve lived in the Garden of Eden, a place of unstained, pure, and untainted beauty, where God met them in the cool of the day to walk and talk.

Paradise was lost with sin. We were meant for paradise, but it's not too late because eternal paradise is found in Jesus Christ. No matter what was done, or what was experienced, the pathway home is through Jesus, for He is the Life, the Truth, and the Way. His loving arms are open wide to all who receive Him. And, when we open our hearts to Jesus, He opens eternal paradise to us.

When I think of talking with God and listening to Him, I see a garden pathway started before the beginning of time, from the garden of Eden to the garden of Gethsemane, to the garden paradise of heaven. Even though the journey here on earth is long and difficult with many problems, we can walk the garden pathway and fellowship with our Savior.

Dear Reader, my prayer is that each page of this devotional will bring truths from God's word to bring encouragement, Godly wisdom, comfort, and joy. Toward the end of the book, I have compiled prayers and verses to help along your journey.

When my voyage is over, I hope to meet you in God's paradise. Until then, my prayers are with you as we travel along the narrow pathway Home.

"And the Lord will continually guide you, and satisfy your soul in scorched and dry places, and give strength to your bones; and you will be like a watered garden, and like a spring of water whose waters do not fail." (Isaiah 58:11, AMP)

A gentle story

Sweet hubby and I watched a movie from the 1940s — a gentle story of a family with all their funny little idiosyncrasies, struggles, hopes, and dreams.

For days, I contemplated the gentleness of the film, the love the family had for one another, and the sacrifices they made through each hardship. Their story gentled my heart.

In a world full of hardships and struggles, we need a gentle story. We need to see that others have made it through pain, misunderstandings, family issues, and life issues. We need a happy ending.

The Bible has the most gentle of stories, the story of One who laid down His all so we could gain all. Jesus Christ through His sacrifice so that all who will come to Him become His family. Jesus grants eternal life and gives His gentle help through the trials and difficulties here on earth.

God hushes storms to gentle whispers and offers to carry our heart-wrenching burdens on His gentle heart. In the family of God, He will help us through the pain, misunderstandings, family issues, our and life issues, and will always bring us to a happy ending.

Heavenly Father, thank You that I'm in Your family. Thank You for Your unfailing love, and You will never leave or forsake me. Thank You that You are an ever-present help in times of trouble. Thank you for loving me even with all my idiosyncrasies, struggles, hopes, and dreams.

Thank You, Heavenly Father, for Your gentle heart that carries me through this crazy world and brings me safely home. Please gentle my heart in You.

"He hushes the storm to a calm and to a gentle whisper, so that the waves of the sea are still." (Psalm 107:29, AMPC)

"Come to Me, all you who labor and are heavy-laden and overburdened, and I will cause you to rest. [I will ease and relieve and refresh your souls.] Take My yoke upon you and learn of Me, for I am gentle (meek) and humble (lowly) in heart, and you will find rest (relief and ease and refreshment and recreation and blessed quiet) for your souls." (Matthew 11:28-29, AMPC)

The frog gift

With a heavy heart, I sat in the grass and pulled weeds. Our sweet little dog, who had blessed our family for fifteen years, had passed away, and I missed Chipper's furry sweetness. In the past, whenever I worked in the yard, he would keep me company. Now, I sat alone and lonely.

I reached for a weed, and a startled frog hopped away. He then turned to look, stopped, and sat down watching me. I wondered if he was the frog several months ago that I had rescued from the washer.

Our dirty yard shoes had been stored on the patio, and I had thrown them in the washer without checking to see if anything was inside. Fortunately, before the cycle began, the Lord prompted me to check in the machine. The frog had popped out of the soapy water, and I rescued and took him back to the yard.

The frog now sat near me, just watching. A few minutes later, content I was safe, he closed his eyes and napped.

The frog was a gift. The sweetness of his trust brought me to tears, and the sweetness of God to bring a friend while I worked made the time even more precious. God knew I was missing Chipper, and God knew I needed a reminder to trust Him.

God is kind and compassionate. He knows when we are hurting and need a reminder of His love. James tells us every good thing given and every perfect gift is from above, coming down from the Father of lights.

God lights the dark places in our souls, the places sad and weary. The lonely places are lit with the reminders we are never forsaken and always loved.

When your days are dark, watch for God's light shining in sweet ways. You are always loved, and His light will always shine.

"Every good thing given, and every perfect gift is from above, coming down from the Father of lights, with whom there is no variation or shifting shadow." (James 1:17, NASB)

I won't force you

I won't force you to love Jesus, but I will beg you. Jesus Christ, Son of God, God in flesh, offers forgiveness, mercy, grace, and eternal life. I've never known a love so pure, so tender, and so wonderful as the love of Jesus. He took my brokenness and made me whole. He restored my life. He forgave me for my sins and helped me forgive others who sinned against me. Jesus took my life and gave me His life.

There is no love like the love of God and His Son, Jesus Christ. No love so great, so amazing. John 3:16 isn't just a sign at the end zone of a football game, it's a verse that is truth. Truth about a love so amazing, so wonderful, so divine.

"God loved the world so much that he gave his one and only Son so that whoever believes in him may not be lost but have eternal life. God did not send his Son into the world to judge the world guilty, but to save the world through him." (John 3:16-17, NCV)

God loved the world, that means you! God is love, so love is inviting you to be loved. He loved you so much that Jesus came to make a way for you to have eternal life. Oh, I want you to come to Jesus. Your heart is forever safe with Him.

When you invite Jesus into your heart, when you tell Him to come into your life, your life changes from the inside out.

His love washes you clean, renews, and recreates you to be the best you that was created to be you.

Oh, I want you to know Jesus. I won't force you, but I will beg you, please don't pass up the opportunity to love Jesus. For when you love Him, you receive His perfect love.

Jesus loves you, will you come to know Jesus's love? I won't force you, but I will beg you. Please come to the love of Jesus.

Journey to The Master's House

Chapter 24 of Genesis tells the story of Abraham sending his servant to find a wife for his son, Isaac. There are so many sweet aspects of the story and many lessons to apply to our lives.

The servant was told to go in the authority of his master, Abraham. – As followers of Jesus, servants, we also are told by Jesus to go in His authority (Matthew 28:18-20).

The servant asked for clarity. — We too can ask for guidance and direction from God through prayer and reading God's word (James 1:5, Psalm 73:24, 2 Timothy 3:16-17).

The servant responded in action. — We also need to be faithful servants (2 Thessalonians 1:11-12, 1 Corinthians 15:57-58, Matthew 25:14-46, Psalm 31:23, Psalm 37:3).

The servant prayed for favor and specific guidance. — We should always pray, praying for favor, specific guidance, and wisdom (1 Thessalonians 5:17, Psalm 90:17, Psalm 25:4, James 1:5).

The servant kept alert, waiting, and watching to see what God would do. – We also should keep alert, watching and waiting to see how God is moving (1 Corinthians 16:13, Habakkuk 2:1, Psalm 27:14).

The servant shared his mission and why he had come. – As followers and servants of Jesus, we are to tell others about Him and make disciples, to share His good news (Matthew 28:19-20, Romans 10:15).

The servant thanked God and rejoiced when His prayers were answered. — We too should be thankful in all things, rejoicing always, telling others of God's faithfulness (Ephesians 5:20, Psalm 75:1, Psalm 40:10).

The servant and Rebekah returned to his master. The bride came to her new home. – We, and those we have told about Jesus and accepted His offer of grace, also will joyfully go to our Master's House as the bride of Christ (Matthew 25:21, John 14:1-3, Revelation 21:3-4), Revelation 22:17).

As believers and followers of Jesus Christ, we have good, good news to share. Go, tell others about Jesus and His wonderful offer of eternal life in heaven.

If you don't know Jesus as Lord and Savior of your life, God's Son, Jesus Christ, offers for you forgiveness, mercy, and eternal life. Open your heart to Jesus, drink deep of His grace, and come home to The Master's House.

"The [Holy] Spirit and the bride (the church, the true Christians) say, Come! And let him who is listening say, Come! And let everyone come who is thirsty [who is painfully conscious of his need of those things by which the soul is refreshed, supported, and strengthened]; and whoever [earnestly] desires to do it, let him come, take, appropriate, and drink the water of Life without cost." (Revelation 22:17, AMPC)

Finding home

Another move loomed on the horizon, and I pondered what it would mean for me and my family. Okay, I'll be honest, it's mainly me I was considering. This would be my thirty-sixth move.

I didn't just want to find another house; I wanted a home.

As we moved again, I wondered if it would be a good place as we continued to get older. Would we have a good church, doctors, and friends, and would the city be a positive and safe place to live?

Regardless of the answers to the questions, I need to remember God is already wherever He sends us. God's presence is home – my eternal home. If I will give myself freely, stop worrying about my needs and focus on God, He will meet all needs according to His riches in glory.

As I give freely of my earthly desire for earthly things, God blesses with more – more of Him! What is given freely, receives God's free gifts with pressed down, poured out blessings. In holding nothing, I receive everything. In losing my life, I find The Life.

God has not given the spirit of fear, we need not worry about anything because our heavenly Father cares about everything (including where the Buffaloe roam).

Amy Carmichael wrote, *"Think of yourself as belonging first to your Lord and then to all, Servant of all. In serving any one of the 'all' you are serving Him who is your Lord. Life is never lonely or empty if we keep Him where He must always be, in the first place.*"[i]

Making the Lord the first place, my first love, surrendering all to Him to be used in His service, that is where Home is found. In His presence is fullness of joy, and with Christ in our hearts, we are already Home.

Is God prompting you to move? Perhaps He isn't directing you to relocate your household, but He is asking you to move forward in a new direction. Whatever place God guides you, wherever He leads, you will find home in His joyful presence.

"You will make known to me the path of life; in Your presence is fullness of joy; in Your right hand there are pleasures forever." (Psalm 16:11, NASB)

I caught it!

Enjoying the warm summer evening, I stood in left field. My softball skills weren't the best, and the coach had placed me where he thought I could do the least damage. But then, with a crack of the bat, the ball zoomed right at me. I held up my glove for self-preservation. With a *whump*, the ball landed safely in my mitt. I jumped for joy and celebrated with all my might. ***I caught it!***

However, my teammates weren't celebrating with me, instead they were yelling. Wasn't catching the ball a good thing? Why was the other team still running? I caught the ball, weren't they supposed to stop?

Unfortunately, I didn't realize I needed to throw the ball back into the field of play until it was too late. The other team scored.

I'm embarrassed by my previous lack of ball skills, and I wish I could tell you I was just a child. The truth is, I was in my twenties playing with people from work. (my softball career ended quickly.).

I know better now. I understand the rules. Catching the ball was only part of the process, throwing it back into play would have kept the other team from scoring. Releasing what I had in my hand would have doubled my joy and definitely made my teammates happier.

When we receive Jesus as Lord of our lives, we are joyfully given His mercy, grace, and eternal life.

When we pass on what we have been freely given, our joy doubles -- we celebrate, heaven celebrates, and the body of Christ celebrates. And, as we share the good news, we also stop the enemy from advancing.

Have you been blessed to receive Jesus as your Savior? Have you caught His grace? Share Jesus and let the celebrations begin!

"...there is joy before the angels of God over one sinner who repents...Go therefore and make disciples of all nations..." Luke 15:10, Matthew 28:19, ESV)

Stuck and trapped

In 1876 a plant known as Kudzu was imported to help with erosion. Those few plants spread like wildfire, their roots shoot out, gripping the ground, crawling, covering trees, houses, and practically envelops anything that stands in its way. The Kudzu root system and interlocking vines become almost impossible to eradicate.

During the early 1980's, I worked for a man who often traveled for his upper-management sales position. George* enjoyed his job and life. After each trip, he returned to the office with fun stories. One of his meetings took place in the deep south. Hungry and tried, George arrived late at night at his hotel. Room service was unavailable, and he didn't have keys to a car since his business partner had rented the automobile.

George looked out his window from the hilltop and noticed a fast-food restaurant. From where he stood, the fastest and easiest route seemed to be across a field. Dressed in his polyester, tan business suit, he made his way across the parking lot and began his journey. Unfortunately, he didn't realize that green field was covered in Kudzu.

Sometime in the night, George's business partner stood on his balcony and heard a plaintive cry for help. In the distance, he noticed a little tan spot in a sea of dark green. Kudzu had intertwined around George's legs and body, and he was unable to move. A rescue team was called to help eradicate him from the grips of the clinging vine.

The way had looked good and seemed to be an easy short cut for George, but he found out the hard way he should have taken the clear road.

Sin often looks like the easy way, a better way, a different way, to get what is wanted, but sin clings, claws, and envelops, sticking the sinner with negative consequences. The sinner is stuck and trapped, helpless without a rescuer and Savior.

I have good news, no matter how stuck your sin situation may seem, Jesus Christ is the rescuer, redeemer, and Savior.

"My little children, I am telling you this so that you will stay away from sin. But if you sin, there is someone to plead for you before the Father. His name is Jesus Christ, the one who is all that is good and who pleases God completely. He is the one who took God's wrath against our sins upon himself and brought us into fellowship with God; and he is the forgiveness for our sins, and not only ours but all the world's." (1 John 2:1-2, TLB)

"What happiness for those whose guilt has been forgiven! What joys when sins are covered over! What relief for those who have confessed their sins and God has cleared their record." (Psalm 32:1-2, TLB)

*Name has been changed.

Invisible hands

During a time of prayer, I saw myself walking and my hands were partially see-through, only a vague outline, visible yet invisible.

Interesting concept – letting go and not holding on. By releasing everything into the care of God; carrying no offenses, no expectations, no anger, worry, or concerns, holding nothing but the Lord, we are given amazing freedom.

Walking forward with hands open and down, realizing whatever is done, whatever is now, whatever will come, needs not be carried but released to God.

By trusting God, giving everything, every burden, to Him, knowing He has the future in His loving hands, we walk unencumbered and free.

How are your hands?

"Cast your burden on the Lord [release it] and He will sustain and uphold you; He will never allow the righteous to be shaken (slip, fall, fail)." (Psalm 55:22, AMP)

"Trust in the Lord with all your heart and do not lean on your own understanding. In all your ways acknowledge Him, and He will make your paths straight." (Proverbs 3:5-6, NASB)

"For I know the plans that I have for you,' declares the Lord, 'plans for welfare and not for calamity to give you a future and a hope." (Jeremiah 29:11, NASB)

Because of One

Have you ever wondered if you, one little person, can make a difference? Please don't let Satan convince you that you are only one person, and one person can't make an impact.

Because of the preaching and ministry of one man, D. L. Moody, perhaps as many as a million people were saved for God's kingdom.

Because of the faith of one woman, Rahab, her family was spared (Joshua 6:25).

Because of the faith of one man, Daniel, a nation turned to God (Daniel 6:26-27).

Because of the faith of one man, Nehemiah, a wall was built (Nehemiah).

Because of one little boy, David, a giant was slain (1 Samuel 17).

Because of one Savior, the world is offered salvation, grace, and eternal life (John 3:16-17).

Because of one person, lives were changed, hope regained, ministries birthed, and encouragement given. Because of one person's obedience, one person's faith, one person's prayer, mighty changes take place in this world.

Because of **The One** who lives within you, nothing is impossible. You are God's unique creation for unique purposes. With Christ living in you, you have the power of all-mighty God within you.

Be the one who prays the powerful prayer.

Be the one who stands up for what is right.

Be the one who stands in the gap.

Be the one who steps out in faith.

Be the one who believes God and follows Him.

Be the one who writes that story, who sends that note, who makes the phone call to share the good news.

Be brave, be strong, be courageous, and be the one who remembers that all things are possible with God.

Because of you, because of the one person created by God, allow Him to freely move in you and watch God work through you in mighty ways.

"Have I not commanded you? Be strong and courageous. Do not be frightened, and do not be dismayed, for the Lord your God is with you wherever you go." (Joshua 1:9, ESV)

Fireflies

Awestruck with wonder, she watched as tiny flashes filled the night sky. Hand outstretched, she squealed in glee as a firefly landed on her small fingers. A dark night transformed into a marvelous soul-pleasing delight.

Our world is a dark place, and we as Christians are here to be fireflies in the darkness. We are bearers of The Good News and have the marvelous light of Christ shining within us. Oh, that we would live in such a way that others are drawn to the wonder and beauty of Jesus Christ.

Be a light, shining in a way that glorifies God. You are a light-bearer, so let your light shine!

"Let your light so shine before men, that they may see your good works and glorify your Father in heaven. Here's another way to put it: You're here to be light, bringing out the God-colors in the world. God is not a secret to be kept. We're going public with this, as public as a city on a hill. If I make you light-bearers, you don't think I'm going to hide you under a bucket, do you? I'm putting you on a light stand. Now that I've put you there on a hilltop, on a light stand—**shine**!"

"...you are a chosen race, a royal priesthood, a holy nation, a people for God's own possession, so that you may **proclaim the excellencies of Him who has called you out of darkness into His marvelous light**. ...walk in a manner worthy of the Lord,   to please Him in all respects, bearing fruit in every good work and increasing in the knowledge of God; strengthened with all power, according to His glorious might, for the attaining of all steadfastness and patience; joyously giving thanks to the Father, who has qualified us to share in the inheritance of the **saints in Light**."(Matthew 5:16, NKJV), Matthew 5:14-15, MSG), 1 Peter 2:9, NASB), Colossians 1:10-12, NASB) (Bold mine)

Wasted steps

My fitness tracker monitors steps taken, calories burned, and other data to help me get in shape. Knowing my movements are being scrutinized has made me more active.

I enjoy seeing how I'm doing each day, especially when the monitor buzzes with excitement when I reach a set goal.

However, if the tracker is off my wrist, I feel like any steps are just wasted because I want to get credit when I move.

My Biblical hero walker is Enoch (see Genesis 5:24). He walked so closely with God that God took him directly to heaven.

Enoch didn't waste any of his steps. In the same way, we need to be careful to properly use the hours given in each day.

Time spent on things that take us away from God and His purposes are fruitless and wasted. Paul reminds us to walk in a manner worthy of the Lord, to run our race, running in such a way to win.

No need to waste steps. Stay plugged into God. Whatever God has called you to do, do it with all your might, walk worthy, and make very step count.

For we are God's workmanship, created in Christ Jesus for good works, which God prepared beforehand that we should walk in them.

Therefore, walk in a manner worthy of the Lord, fully pleasing to Him: bearing fruit in every good work and increasing in the knowledge of God; being strengthened with all power, according to His glorious might, for all endurance and patience with joy (Ephesians 2:10, Colossians 1:10-11).

Be the change

Anyone else troubled by the number of murders and rising crime rate? I am! Thankfully I realized we are not left helpless. James tells us, "The earnest (heartfelt, continued) prayer of a righteous man makes tremendous power available [dynamic in its working]." (James 5:16, AMPC)

No matter who you are, where you live, how old or young, regardless of social status, you have an opportunity to be the change. As Christians, we are given *amazing* power to fight against the enemy. The battles we face, the fight around us are not with flesh and blood. Satan and his demons are in the world trying to mess up the world. However, we are given **God's power** <u>through Christ</u>, who has **all** authority and power, to fight any and every battle.

God is greater than anyone or anything in the world, and with Jesus living within us, we have HIS power. Our prayers are powerful because our God is **ALL-POWERFUL!**

Use the power you've been given in Christ. Pray for revival. Pray blind eyes will be opened; hearts will be drawn to Christ, and the power of the enemy broken. Pray for your city and country. Prayer-walk your home and neighborhood and pray for those who live and work near you.

Be the undercurrent that brings the current of change. Mustard seed sized faith moves mountains, and one person's prayer can be the spark that ignites revival.

Throughout history, many of the major revivals can be traced back to the prayers of one person or just a few people. Satan wants us to be so worried and concerned that we don't do anything but be worried and concerned. Let's use the power of prayer. Prayers make a difference and have power to bring about change. Pray for God's Spirit to move. Pray God's word to fight against the evil in the world.

Pray that men and women of God will stand firm, be bold, and accurately teach God's word. Pray for God's truth to expose the enemy's lies. Pray as God's Spirit leads you to pray. Pray, friends. Pray, and watch God work!

Heavenly Father, I humbly come before You. Thank You that You are all-powerful, loving and a just God. I praise and thank You that nothing is hidden from You and nothing is impossible for You. Oh Father, there is so much evil in the world and so much heartache. Please open the eyes of those blinded by the enemy, open them to see You, to hear Your truth, and to turn their hearts to You.

Pour out Your Holy Spirit on our land, shine Your light and expose the lies of Satan. Raise up Your children to live to please You and boldly live for You. Show us clearly how to love with Your love. Holy Spirit guide us in our prayers so that You can freely move in our lives and in our world. We love You, Father and ask these things in the name of Your Son, Jesus Christ. Amen.

Strengthen the core

While in physical therapy for compressed discs in my neck, the therapist reminded me to make a conscious effort to keep my stomach muscles tight. Those muscles are vital to many common movements, such as lifting, twisting, reaching, and bending. A weak core causes problems with posture, back and neck pain, and other health-related issues.

This made me wonder if my spiritual core is strong. Spiritual core muscles are strengthened by spending time with God, reading and remembering His truth. Our spiritual muscles won't be strengthened without a conscious effort.

The world is a rough place, and if we don't have a strong spiritual core, we will be tossed and tumbled like a pebble in the ocean. Our firm foundation is on the solid rock of Christ. He is Truth and His truth helps us stand strong.

To keep our spiritual core strong...

Read and memorize God's word. His word is a lamp for our feet and a light for our path. All scripture is inspired by God, profitable for teaching, for reproof, for correction and for training in righteousness.

Spend time with God in prayer. Pray as the Holy Spirit leads you to pray. Pray for the things needed. Watch and keep on praying. Remember to pray for the lost and for other Christians.

Spiritual exercise takes effort. Build yourselves up in your faith, praying in the Holy Spirit, staying in the love of God.

Lay aside everything that hinders and the sin that entangles, run with endurance the race set before you by fixing your eyes on Jesus. Run to win the prize, stir up and rekindle the flame the inner fire within you. Remember you were not given the spirit of timidity, cowardice, or fear but God has given power, love, a calm and well-balanced mind, discipline and self-control.

Work out your salvation using God's strength and energy, and He will fulfill your purpose for His good pleasure. Remember God is in control, and nothing is impossible for Him.

Terrible things happen in this difficult world, but God sees all, His ears are attentive to the cries of the righteous. God will give to each what their deeds deserve, and He will punish evil.

Perfect peace comes from the stability of our unfailing, unchanging, ever-loving God. Fix your thoughts on Him, trust in Him always. Always trust in God.

Finally, "exercise daily in God—no spiritual flabbiness, please! Workouts in the gymnasium are useful, but a disciplined life in God is far more so, making you fit both today and forever. You can count on this. Take it to heart. ... We're banking on the living God, Savior of all men and women...." (1 Timothy 4:8-10, MSG)

2 Timothy 3:16, Psalm 119:105, Ephesians 6:18, Jude 1:20-21, Hebrews 12:1-2, 1 Corinthians 9:24. 2 Timothy 1:6-7, Philippians 2:12-13, Psalm 46:10 Luke 1:37, Proverbs 15:3, Psalm 34:15-16, Isaiah 13:11, Romans 2:5-9, Isaiah 26:3-4

Trouble Inoculation

In need of God's wisdom and guidance, I knelt in the yard to pray and pull weeds. Working in the soil gives me a hands-on visual of removing weedy thoughts.

Concerned about a possible encounter with someone, I prayed God would teach me what I needed in advance of what I thought might happen. As I prayed and pondered, I realized God's ways and thoughts are higher than the heavens and my understanding is always extremely limited. But, to be honest, I was hoping God would download any information needed in advance and prepare me with a trouble inoculation.

The situation I'm imagining may not even happen, but if it does, I don't need to worry, God and His provision will already be in place. God knows our thoughts; He knows what we've been through and what we will go through. He created each of us and knows how to respond to our unique personalities and unique needs.

Are you worried about the future? No need for a trouble inoculation. God is timeless and is never surprised at the future. The Lord gives His wisdom and will provide for every need.

Just as Pony Express riders in the old west were given a fresh horse and supplies for each leg of their journey, whatever is needed, whatever will come, whatever trouble may be on the horizon, God's supplies are already in place.

"If any of you lacks wisdom, let him ask God, who gives generously to all without reproach, and it will be given him." (James 1:5, ESV)

29   We Were Meant for Paradise

Gong

Lies, negativity, false reports make me angry and upset. I tell you there are days I want to say something. Grrrr, I really want to chastise people. Fortunately, the Holy Spirit reminds me if I don't have love I'm just a noisy gong or clanging cymbal, and these days there are way too many gongs and cymbals.

No one needs to hear more negative news; they need the eternal positive Good News. So, like David, "I said, I will guard my ways that I may not sin with my tongue; I will guard my mouth as with a muzzle while the wicked are in my presence" (Psalm 39:1).

And I need to remember, "A gentle answer deflects anger, but harsh words make tempers flare." (Proverbs 15:1, NLT)

If I want things to change I need to do things God's way. Prayer is powerfully effective, and through prayers great things happen. Faith moves mountains, nothing is impossible for God, and love conquers all. God's way is the only right and true way. God's way is the only right and true way, and His way brings the world hope, grace, mercy, and eternal life.

Join me in prayer?

Heavenly Father, the world is evil, noisy, and very difficult. Please open the eyes of the blind, soften hard hearts, expose the lies of the enemy, and bring the lost to You. I am so grateful You are always in control, and nothing is impossible for You.

Oh Father, help me to act in faith and come to You in prayer before I say a word. Help me to gently speak and act in Your love. And, "let the words of my mouth and the meditation of my heart be acceptable in Your sight, O Lord, my strength and my Redeemer." (Psalm 19:14, NKJV)

"...When a believing person prays, great things happen. Elijah was a human being just like us. He prayed that it would not rain, and it did not rain on the land for three and a half years!" (James 5:16-17, NCV)

"Jesus answered, 'Because your faith is too small. I tell you the truth, if your faith is as big as a mustard seed, you can say to this mountain, 'Move from here to there,' and it will move. All things will be possible for you.'" (Matthew 17:20, NCV)

"If I could speak all the languages of earth and of angels, but didn't love others, I would only be a noisy gong or a clanging cymbal." (1 Corinthians 13:1, NLT)

"Love is patient and kind. Love is not jealous or boastful or proud or rude. It does not demand its own way. It is not irritable, and it keeps no record of being wronged. It does not rejoice about injustice but rejoices whenever the truth wins out. Love never gives up, never loses faith, is always hopeful, and endures through every circumstance." (1 Corinthians 13:4-7, NLT)

Flip side

Curious, I picked up the gray rock with the smooth, round surface on one side and a flat surface on the other. Nothing seemed special about the dull rock, until I turned it overexposing the inside filled with beautiful, dazzling purple crystals. The flip side changed the dull into beauty.

There's always a flip side.

The devil wants us to focus on the negative, what we don't have so we will not be satisfied with what we do have. Satan also wants us to focus on what we have – an illness, a loss, our trials, and difficulties -- to keep us from any satisfaction. The enemy never wants us to look at the other side and see how God is working.

God loves His children, and all things work together for good to those who love God, to those who are the called according to His purpose (Romans 8:28).

God's ways and purposes are often working beyond our human vision. Nothing is impossible for God; He restores and redeems and makes all things new. The hard-rock life, changes to beauty in the hands of Jesus - The Rock.

Ask God to reveal the flip side, to show you how He is working, to reveal the beauty now and the beauty to come. Rejoice, take heart, there is always a flip side.

"I love you, O Lord, my strength. The Lord is my rock and my fortress and my deliverer, my God, my rock, in whom I take refuge, my shield, and the horn of my salvation, my stronghold. I call upon the Lord, who is worthy to be praised, and I am saved from my enemies." (Psalm 18:1-3, ESV)

Preach!

Billy Graham worked diligently as a minister for God's kingdom, preaching throughout the world to call people to Jesus Christ. Most of us will never reach crowds as large or stand on a platform proclaiming the good news. However, we all have a calling to preach the good news.

We are saved into God's family, to help point others to God's family. Every one of us is called to be a minister and preach the good news of Jesus Christ's saving grace and mercy.

You don't have to be on a stage, your platform is where God has placed you on this planet. All around you are opportunities -- the child in your care, the employees around you, the person behind the counter, the medical staff, your social connections, your family. Every person you meet is a person you can love with the love of Christ and tell them of the love of Christ.

We are ambassadors for Christ, royal proclaiming priests, evangelists, preaching the good news, living in the here and now to help point others to eternal life. Preach Christ to those who know Christ. Preach Christ to those who don't know Christ until they know they need Christ.

We have good news, friends. Let's tell others! Preach!

"Preach the word; be ready in season and out of season; reprove, rebuke, exhort, with great patience and instruction." (2 Timothy 4:2, NASB)

Beyond understanding

I tend to try and figure out things. I want to understand what happened in the past, what I need to do today, and what might happen in the future. I try to reason based on my own reasoning, which leads to basic non-understanding because how can I with my limited understanding understand all things? *Whew*.

The only One who understands everything is God. He is the only One who has knowledge of the past, present, and future. I don't have to understand or have answers to everything, I can trust God who has the understanding and answers for all things.

Happy sigh....

Heavenly Father, help me to trust You for everything and all things. I'm laying my worries, concerns, and troubled mind at Your feet. Thank You that Your peace transcends my understanding. Thank You that You guard my heart and mind. Thank You that You understand all things., and therefore I can trust You with all things.

"Trust in the Lord with all your heart and do not lean on your own understanding. Do not fret or have any anxiety about anything, but in every circumstance and in everything, by prayer and petition (definite requests), with thanksgiving, continue to make your wants known to God. And God's peace [shall be yours, that tranquil state of a soul assured of its salvation through Christ, and so fearing nothing from God and being content with its earthly lot of whatever sort that is, that peace] which transcends all understanding shall garrison and mount guard over your hearts and minds in Christ Jesus." (Proverbs 3:5, NASB), Philippians 4:6-7, AMPC)

The Invitation

Oh, how I wanted to talk to God, to share something deep in my heart, to find the reasons behind my anxious and troubled mind. I wanted to pray, but for some reason couldn't find the words. I've had amazing times in prayer, but something blocked me, a hindrance kept my soul from reaching out.

The Holy Spirit prompted me to read a book on prayer by E.M. Bounds. E.M. Bounds was a mighty man of prayer, and I've read most of his books. I stopped into our church bookstore and on the shelf waited several of his works I already have at home, but then I saw one, a big one (a 622-page book) I had not read. As I pondered whether or not to spend the money, the Lord reminded me He had given me provision.

I purchased the book, and I'm diving in deep to the beauty of prayer, the absolute amazing privilege and blessing of prayer. My soul is singing with joy. As I'm reading and taking notes, praying, enjoying being in God's presence, I realized that the desire to be in communion with God, is actually His desire.

The Father is the One who draws souls to Him. He is the One beckoning us deeper by making our souls desire Him deeper. Draw near to God and He will draw near to you (John 6:44, James 4:8).

Prayer is a divine invitation to meet with The Divine.

E. M. Bounds wrote, *"the heart leaps to meet with God."*

Oh yes, my heart is leaping to meet with my Heavenly Father --- wide open, full-abandoned, no agenda other than to meet with my God. Oh, what joy! What total joy to be abandoned to God!

Do you have a desire to pray more, to commune with God? Those desires are God's desires for you. God is calling to your soul to come meet with Him. He is drawing you close so that Your soul can find rest, peace, guidance, and joy in Him.

The Divine Invitation is addressed to you. "Call to Me and I will answer you, and I will tell you great and mighty things, which you do not know." (Jeremiah 33:3, NASB)

Will you come? Will you answer His invitation?

"My heart has heard you say, 'Come and talk with me.' And my heart responds, 'Lord, I am coming.'" (Psalm 27:8, NLT)

Blessing dance party

Years ago, I worked with a man who was an avid hunter. During one of his hunting trips, he climbed a tree, tied himself to the trunk, and kept watch. After several hours, his eyes grew heavy, and he fell asleep. When he woke, he looked down to discover a plethora of hoof prints circling the base of the tree. I imagine a herd of deer, walking up, seeing a large snoring hunter, and in response having a dance party while he slept.

Makes me wonder how often in life I've grown weary, closed my eyes, and failed to notice how God was working. James tells us every good thing given and every perfect gift is from our Heavenly Father (James 1:17). God's blessings constantly flow from His throne, but so few pay attention. I want to do better.

I'm finding the more I notice God's blessings, the more I see God's blessings, and the more I notice and see, the more grateful I am. And the more grateful I am, the more I notice, which leads to more noticing, seeing, and gratefulness.

I can even take my hunter friend's misadventure on another fun twist. Our Heavenly Father is greater than any enemy and Satan is a defeated foe. So, we can be like the deer having a dance party because the devil is bound and conquered.

Even through the difficulties of life, God's goodness and blessings keep on flowing. Pray for eyes to see and notice the blessings of God and get ready to dance.

Let us not forget

Instead of wringing hands, crying, and whining, let us not forget that a Godly prayer has the power of God. Pray in God's power, for God to move in His power.

"I have no doubt that much of our praying fails for lack of persistence. So many of our prayers are said without the fire and strength of perseverance. ... men must be in earnest when they kneel at God's footstool." ~ E. M. Bounds[i]

Let us pray for the lost to come to know Jesus Christ. Let us pray for the spiritually blind to receive sight. Let us pray for those who would rather argue, fuss, and fight, that they might be drawn to the One who is gentle and meek and will save their souls. Let us pray for hard hearts to be melted by the love of Christ.

"The potency of prayer has subdued the strength of fire; it has bridled the rage of lions, hushed anarchy to rest, extinguished wards, appeased the elements, expelled demons, burst the chains of death, expanded the gates of heaven, assuaged diseases, repelled frauds, rescued cities from destruction, stayed the sun in its course, and arrested the progress of the thunderbolt. Prayer is an all-efficient panoply, a treasure undiminished, a mine that is never exhausted, a sky unobscured by clouds, a heaven unruffled by the storm. It is the root, the fountain, the mother of a thousand blessings." ~ St. Chrysostom

Let us pray the body of Christ awakens and will arise to be the hands and feet of Jesus. Let us pray we do not faint or grow weary.

Let us pray for God's wisdom and guidance. Let us pray for God to move and be free to move among the nations, that God's light will shine on this dark world.

"*Great things for God are done by great prayers.*" ~ *E. M. Bounds*

Let us not forget that God is always in control, and nothing is impossible for God. Let us pray. Let us pray. Let us pray.

"*In God's name, I beseech you, let prayer nourish your soul as your meals nourish your body. Let your fixed seasons of prayer keep you in God's presence through the day, and may His presence frequently remembered through it be an ever fresh spring of prayer. Such a brief, loving recollection of God renews a man's whole being, quiets his passions, supplies light and counsel in difficulty, gradually subdues the temper, and causes him to possess his soul in patience, or rather gives it up to the possession of God.*" ~ Fénelon

"Pray without ceasing." (1 Thessalonians 5:17, NKJV)

Pray friends, pray!

Defying gravity

The other day while listening to praise music, caught up in the joy of worship, I felt as though my hair was standing on end (Really! I even checked.) No outward signs were showing, but what delight as my spirit soared to the heavens. My feet were touching earth but my soul defied gravity.

Paul said as Christians we are seated in the heavens with Christ (Ephesians 2:5-6). Jesus said the truth will set us free (John 8:32). If I could truly grasp the truth that my soul lives in the heavens, my soul-feet would never touch the ground. I would be walking on air – Holy Spirit air.

We are to love the Lord with all our heart, soul, mind, and strength. In loving God with everything within us, we find we don't want or need anything but God. We find we have all we need in Him and thus defy gravity.

Through praise and worship, filling our thoughts with God's Word, meditating on the goodness of our God, we defy gravity.

The world brings us down and depresses, but loving God presses our hearts into the safety, joy, and peace of His unfailing love. We are never earth-bound when we are heaven-bound (no spacesuit needed to defy gravity).

Always remember Whose you are, and where you are seated. Praise God and defy gravity!

"Praise the Lord! Praise the Lord from the heavens; praise him in the heights!" (Psalm 148:1, ESV)

Instead of complaining...

Instead of complaining, marching, and rioting about an issue, may I suggest doing something helpful? We reap what we sow, so instead of sowing discord, sow seeds to sprout life. Donate your money, your time, and your prayers. Every negative problem is an opportunity for positive change.

Instead of complaining, respond in love. All around you are ways to make a positive impact.

We are blessed to live in a time where we can immediately see and respond to needs around the world. Through your church and other ministries, you can find people actively involved to help respond to those in need.

Many fine organizations and ministries are actively involved in issues around the world. Pray for them to be good stewards and meet the needs of the nations in Christ's name. Pray, donate and get involved in ways that you can.

What has God laid on your heart? How can you join to help?

"If a brother or sister is without clothes and lacks daily food and one of you says to them, 'Go in peace, keep warm, and eat well,' but you don't give them what the body needs, what good is it?" (James 2:15-16, HCSB)

43   We Were Meant for Paradise

Trust Me for the best

Several months ago, the Lord shared in my spirit some amazing and wonderful things that would come soon. With excitement and anticipation, I scurried about the house preparing for what I believed were our next steps. But then, surgeries for us both put a stop on any plans. As health issues slowed us to snails, at times I wondered if I correctly heard God.

Mixed emotions come with every move. After thirty plus moves, you would think it would be easier. However, questions about logistics are ever-present, and the concerns for all required to move to any new location. Can we easily sell the home were in, find an affordable home in another city, locate a good church, find doctors, friends, etc.? All that messes with my head because moving is not easy! The negative what ifs were far outweighing the positive what ifs.

I sensed a heavenly sadness in how I viewed this possible change. Why was I thinking the worst possibilities instead of thinking the best? Why was I not trusting God?

God's love is unfailing. God is a good, good Father who wants the best for His children. God works all things for the good for those who love Him and are called according to His purpose. God knows the plans He has for us, plans for a good future filled with hope. So why look for the negatives instead of the positives? Why am I not leaping in joy that God is leading? Why am I not trusting God for His best?

Oh, my attitude made me so sad. My good, good Father shared amazing things, and I wasn't rejoicing every moment at what is to come.

Oh Father, please forgive me. Forgive me for my negative thinking, for my worries, and lack of trust. Forgive me for not trusting You for the best. Refocus my focus back on Your goodness. Retrain my brain to rejoice in Your faithful, unfailing love. I will stand and watch to see what You will do and how You will lead. I trust You for the best, for You are the best!

"Let me hear of your unfailing love each morning, for I am trusting you. Show me where to walk, for I give myself to you. The Lord is my strength and shield. I trust him with all my heart. He helps me, and my heart is filled with joy. I burst out in songs of thanksgiving." (Psalm 143:8, NLT), Psalm 28:7, NLT)

"Behold, I am doing a new thing! Now it springs forth; do you not perceive and know it and will you not give heed to it? I will even make a way in the wilderness and rivers in the desert." (Isaiah 43:19, AMPC)

"'I say this because I know what I am planning for you,' says the Lord. 'I have good plans for you, not plans to hurt you. I will give you hope and a good future.'" (Jeremiah 29:11, NCV)

Field Plowers

What if you plowed a 100,000-acre field with a team of horses and no one seemed to notice or care? What if you didn't even know if the seeds you planted would sprout and bear a harvest?

Many of our fellow Christian workers feel this way. They plow the fields preaching, teaching, writing, delivering messages of hope and encouragement, but few people ever stop to say thanks.

Barnabas was known as the Son of Encouragement (Acts 4:36). Can you imagine being known as an encourager? What an honor and blessing for all concerned, but I wonder how many people encouraged Barnabas.

Please remember to thank the field plowers, the workers, those who follow Christ and point us to follow Christ. Please remember to encourage others. One word, one pat on the back, one hug, one letter, one email, one thank you, provides strength, hope, and motivation.

Be an encourager to those in Christian ministry and also encourage your brothers and sisters in Christ. Encourage the young mom or dad working to raise her family, the waitress, waiter, the worker at the office or behind the counter. Encourage those who are homebound. Encourage those in civil service, in the military, at home and overseas. Every person you meet, needs encouragement.

We're all in this world together, plowing along in our fields.

Let's wave across the fences, pass a cool glass of water, and encourage one another to keep going for Christ.

"So, speak encouraging words to one another. Build up hope so you'll all be together in this, no one left out, no one left behind. I know you're already doing this; just keep on doing it. And now, friends, we ask you to honor those leaders who work so hard for you, who have been given the responsibility of urging and guiding you along in your obedience. Overwhelm them with appreciation and love!" (1 Thessalonians 5:11-13, MSG)

Show me the lie

Have you ever been troubled and fearful about something? Perhaps even anxious and worried, and didn't even know why you were anxious and worried? Boy, I have.

Sometimes worry, fear, anxiety, and trouble, jump on my back or nip at my heels, and I have no idea how to fix them or sometimes even figure out what is causing all the craziness. Ack! Whimper. Ack!!!!

Difficult and downright scary problems come into our lives. However, Jesus tells us not to worry because our Heavenly Father is a loving, good Father and will always provide for our needs (Matthew 6:25-34).

I believe that, I know those truths. I know God is good and loving, however, Satan is sneaky and knows where to hit. A head-long enemy attack is usually obvious, so the devil often uses bothersome and downright crazy, annoying problems that surround like gnats buzzing around our heads or like gerbils nipping at our heels.

Satan is out to steal, kill, and destroy. As Christians, the enemy can't take away our salvation, but he will try to steal our joy and hope, kill our passion for Christ, and destroy our witness.

Behind every fear, worry and anxiety, is a demonic lie. Satan wants us to believe in the midst of our problems, in the middle of storms, God is not sufficient, not powerful enough, not loving enough, and won't help.

The Truth is God is loving, ALL-powerful, ALL-sufficient, just and righteous, and He takes care of His children.

"Freedom from spiritual conflicts and bondage is not a power encounter; it's a truth encounter. Satan is a deceiver, and he will work undercover at all costs. But the truth of God's Word exposes him and his lies." (Neil T. Anderson[ii]

To get back on the solid ground of Truth, remember who God is, remember His promises and His Word. During battles, go to God and ask Him, "What is the lie the enemy has planted in my head?"

I've found lies range from unbelief, distrust in God's love and sufficiency, worries about our inadequacy, and many others. Our battle is not with flesh and blood, behind the mess is Satan making all the mess.

Therefore, let's ask the Holy Spirit to reveal God's truth. His truth sets us free, and the Word of God is our offensive weapon. You are never left defenseless. Go to God, ask Him to show you the lie, then combat that lie with God's truth.

Pray with me?

Heavenly Father, please show me the lie behind this battle. Reveal Your truth so I may stand firm on Your truth and combat every enemy lie. Help me to find scriptures I can pray about each situation. Open my eyes to see beyond the person, situation, or circumstance that seems to be causing the problems.

Heavenly Father, show me the lie the enemy has planted, and then help me to remember Your truth and quiet me with Your love. There is nothing too hard for You, nothing is impossible for You, for You are ALL-mighty and forever loving. You will never leave me or forsake me. Thank You, Father, that in Your light and truth, every enemy will fall.

I ask these things in the name of Your Son, Jesus Christ, who is my Savior. Amen.

"For our struggle is not against flesh and blood [contending only with physical opponents], but against the rulers, against the powers, against the world forces of this [present] darkness, against the spiritual forces of wickedness in the heavenly (supernatural) places. Therefore, put on the complete armor of God, so that you will be able to [successfully] resist and stand your ground in the evil day [of danger], and having done everything [that the crisis demands], to stand firm [in your place, fully prepared, immovable, victorious]." (Ephesians 6:12-13, AMP)

"The Lord your God is in your midst, a victorious warrior. He will exult over you with joy, He will be quiet in His love, He will rejoice over you with shouts of joy." (Zephaniah 3:17, NASB)

Jesus said, "If you continue in My word, then you are truly disciples of Mine; and you will know the truth, and the truth will make you free." (John 8:31-32, NASB)

He's holding out on you

Waiting. Waiting for prayers to be answered, waiting for a move to take place, waiting for change to come, waiting for the prodigal to return home, waiting for healing... waiting.

Hope flickers and starts to fade; hands barely hold on. Then, comes a sinister whisper, *"God's holding out on you. If God loved you, your prayers would be answered."* Satan plants doubts in hearts and minds that God is withholding something needed, wanted, or desired.

The devil would love for us to doubt God. Adam and Eve believed Satan's lies that God was holding out on them, and we know how that turned out.

As I prayed again this morning, so hoping this would be the day our wait would be over, the healing would come, the right choices made, I realized I don't just want God's good, I want God's best. I want His best for my friends and family members, I want His best for all concerned.

Throughout the Bible, people had to wait, but then amazing things happened -- seas parted, enemies defeated, and dead were raised to life. Waiting on God brings spiritual growth as our faith is stretched and our hearts are prepared for the next steps. We are prepared and the future needs are prepared.

God is not holding out on us when He has us wait, He's preparing His best. God is love, He is just and righteous, His plans are the best. Wait for God. Trust Him, for the best is yet to come.

Are you waiting and your hope is fading? Is the enemy taunting you that God is holding out on you? Remember the truth that God's love is unfailing, and He never withholds the best for His children.

"The Lord takes delight in his faithful followers, and in those who wait for his loyal love. Wait for the Lord; be strong and let your heart take courage; yes, wait for the Lord. For the Lord God is a sun and shield; the Lord gives grace and glory; no good thing does He withhold from those who walk uprightly." (Psalm 147:11, NET Bible), Psalm 27:14, NASB), Psalm 84:11, NASB)

Joy search

Sad, weary, and tired, I prayed for joy.

Unfortunately, joy didn't return, and I wasn't sure what I needed to do, so I continued to pray and ponder what had happened, what went wrong, why I didn't feel super-joyful all the time.

Then, I read about a Christian author, a "melancholy person" who responded to a young woman who had asked for help in finding her joy. The author replied, "why not try another mood." At first, I sat there puzzled. I had never considered moods coming and going like seasons, that it was okay to have down-times and up-times.

I'm old enough to know seasons do come with times of joy and times that feel dry and lifeless. Life is hard, sometimes boring and monotonous, often difficult, with a variety of challenges each day. There is a time for every season.

I need to embrace God, not a feeling or emotion. I need to embrace God who never changes. The burden of "finding joy" rolled off my shoulders.

God's joy is constant, His joy continuously flows from His throne. His joy is not hindered by my actions or inactions. The joy of the Lord is our strength. HIS joy, not mine, not yours, not theirs, His joy is always constant and the source of unending strength for every moment of every day.

Even when the mood changes, God's joy remains. Regardless of the season, regardless of the mood, we can rest knowing His joy remains. And, His joy is available for us. Oh my, what joy! ☺

Whatever emotion you are feeling, remember God's joy is forever flowing from His throne to bless, encourage, and strengthen you.

"I have told you these things so that My joy and delight may be in you, and that your joy may be made full and complete and overflowing." (John 15:11, AMP)

"...Do not be grieved, for the joy of the LORD is your strength." (Nehemiah 8:10, ESV)

Ya gotta get the wood!

I busied myself during the day, praying and hoping God would download a marvelous devotion for me to share. I prayed, completed my Bible study, worked in the yard, cleaned house, cooked meals, prayed, stared at the computer and still nothing came. My days were hit and miss with revelation of something worthy to share.

I kept wondering what was wrong. Had my calling as a writer changed? Did some sin in my life block the Holy Spirit? I prayed, begged, pleaded, repented, prayed, and still I seemed to be sputtering instead of moving forward.

Then I remembered the words Paul had written to Timothy to "stir up (rekindle the embers of, fan the flame of, and keep burning) the [gracious] gift of God, [the inner fire] that is in you." Also "study and do your best to present yourself to God approved, a workman [tested by trial] who has no reason to be ashamed, accurately handling and skillfully teaching the word of truth."

Oh! I needed to rekindle the embers and fan into flame to get my writing going again. Then I wondered what did I have for kindling?

Oh yes, I gotta get the wood!

Most of what I was doing was good, but I had missed a primary thing. I needed to get my tail in the chair and get to work. God has prompted and gifted me to write, but I must use that ability and actually write.

Ah, yes when you want to start a fire, ya gotta get the wood. I believe the Lord has called me to share His good news with others. However, thinking about doing something, praying about doing something, and actually doing something is very different. Prayer and Bible study are most important, but I also need to keep my fire burning, and do my best to present myself to God as His workman and use His gift by keeping my tail in my writing chair and writing.

We are all gifted by God, each of us are given gifts, talents, and blessings (see Romans 12:6-11 and 1 Corinthians 12:4-11).

What has God called you to do? How has God gifted you? Keep your fires burning by remembering to use the gifts He has given you for His glory.

2 Timothy 1:6, AMPC; 2 Timothy 2:15, AMP)

Jesus is in the house!

Jesus "entered Capernaum after some days, and it was heard that He was in the house." (Mark 2:1, NKJV)

Jesus was in the house and people came from far and wide to see Him. The house was packed, so very crowded no one else could get inside. However, that didn't stop four men from tearing through the roof to bring their paralyzed friend to Jesus. Because when Jesus is in the house, lives are changed.

When Jesus is in our house (our hearts), change happens. As our lives change, others notice. And oh, that people would see and say, Jesus is in that house!

Allow Jesus in your heart so that others are drawn to open their hearts to Jesus.

Is Jesus in your house?

"God is love. When we take up permanent residence in a life of love, we live in God and God lives in us. This way, love has the run of the house, becomes at home and mature in us..." (1 John 4:17-18, MSG)

"May the God who gives endurance and encouragement give you the same attitude of mind toward each other that Christ Jesus had, so that with one mind and one voice you may glorify the God and Father of our Lord Jesus Christ." (Romans 15:5-6, NIV)

Waiting well

I've been in a quiet place, a place where at times I'm crazy desperate to know what's next. I sense I'm in a waiting room, a seemingly dark waiting room. I don't care for the dark, and some days I do not wait well. Can anyone else identify? Is it just me?

In the past, the Lord used illness and surgeries to cause me to slow down and stop. Those times were the worst of times and the best of times; they were hard, horribly painful, but came with the beautiful blessings of soul-healing. When all you can do is spend time with The One who made you, that time is good, very good.

Now that my body is doing pretty well, I'm watching and waiting to move forward. To be honest, I know I'm only confined by myself, only crazy nuts in the wait because I have a tendency to be crazy and nuts. I want to *see* the next step! Please... Whimper... please, Lord?

In this strange time of waiting and at times flailing, I'm sensing God at work. He's stripping away things I didn't even know were weighing me down. He's teaching me lessons, even though most days I didn't recognize I sat in His classroom.

Many times, I've pictured I'm in a small, confining, difficult place to stand. Yet in the confinement of a wait, God enlarges the step. The steps may seem small through human eyes, but they are never wasted, they are full and free for training, revelation, intimacy, and joy with the Lord.

Waiting isn't always a negative thing. If I want something, I would prefer that something as soon as possible. However, if I am crossing a river full of crocodiles, I would be very happy to delay until any large-tooth critters are gone or occupied with something else.

Waiting is often a preparation, a getting rid of the things we don't need on the next part of our journey, a soul-stilling to have the soul tuned in to God to prepare our soul for what God has planned.

I'm waiting and I want to wait well. Amy Carmichael wrote, *"Blessed are the single-hearted, for they shall enjoy much peace. If you refuse to be hurried and pressed, if you stay your soul on God, nothing can keep you from that clearness of spirit which is life and peace. In that stillness you will know what His will is."*

Are you waiting? Stay your soul on God. Be still. Rest and know, you are always safe in God's hands, and soon you will know His will.

Be still, the Lord rescues, the Lord fights for His children (Exodus 14:14).

Be still, wait patiently (Psalm 37:7).

Be still and know that He is God (Psalm 46:10).

Be still, He calms the storm (Mark 4:39).

Be still...

"Do you not know? Have you not heard? The Lord is the everlasting God, the Creator of the ends of the earth. He will not grow tired or weary, and his understanding no one can fathom. He gives strength to the weary and increases the power of the weak.

Even youths grow tired and weary, and young men stumble and fall; but those who hope in the Lord will renew their strength. They will soar on wings like eagles; they will run and not grow weary, they will walk and not be faint." (Isaiah 40:28-31, NIV)

No sugar-coated fluff

Sweet hubby and I were very proud of ourselves for eating healthy. Unfortunately, I quietly went to my office, shut the door, and ate a stash of candy.

The result? My body was not happy, resulting in a sick stomach and regret at my failure. Ugh. I should have stayed with the healthy food groups.

Spiritually, I need protein. Sugar-coated fluff doesn't feed my inner spirit. There's nothing wrong with lighthearted reading, but to grow and stay spiritually healthy, I need proper spiritual food.

When I'm in a battle, I need to read the Bible and books that help me know how to battle. God's word along with saints who have gone before us, who lived in this embattled world, have left behind stories of their journey to help us along our journey.

The Word of God shows us how to wear spiritual armor and gives truth to set us free. God's word is fire and a hammer that shatters rock, burning away the lies of the enemy and shattering misconceptions and misinformation. His Word is living and active, sharper than a two-edged sword, getting to the heart of the matter to help our thoughts and hearts stand firm in every matter.

Read God's Word, let His words fill your body, mind, heart, and soul with His truth and the knowledge of His unfailing love and power. Read and memorize the Bible, pray God's word and live in God's Word, for His word is healing, restoration, strength, and life.

Are you feeling spiritually anemic? Pick up spiritual protein by reading the Bible and other books that bring you closer to God's heart and nurture your faith.

"Every word of God proves true; he is a shield to those who take refuge in him." (Proverbs 30:5, ESV)

Jeremiah 23:29, Proverbs 30:5, Hebrews 4:12, Matthew 4:4

Still waiting

Waiting is not easy. My body can be sitting still but my brain races in a thousand different directions. I want to figure out each step and what that step may mean and where the next step will lead. Life becomes all about me; thinking I have to perform and do and be, and jump through hoops, and pray, and analyze, and do, do, do, do as much as I can do, instead of resting and trusting.

I far too often forget God's ways are higher than I can even imagine. Who would have thought having Gideon whittle down his army from over 30,000 to only 300 men, then arming them with torches and pitchers would be the way to triumph over an army of over 100,000?

Who would have thought marching around a fortified city for seven days then shouting would have brought down a huge protective wall?

Who would have thought a couple WAY past their child-bearing years would have fathered a nation?

Who would have thought a virgin would give birth to the King?

Nothing is impossible for God; logic can only be seen from the only logical viewpoint -- God's viewpoint. He sees the eternal perspective unclouded by time and human understanding.

We can't see the workings, answers, and solutions working in the heavenly cosmos. Solutions often don't make sense in our time structure because the structure, the target is fluid, beautifully fluid to a beautifully God-orchestrated ending.

Through the suffering, through the pain, through the wait, comes refining and preparation and a beautiful tapestry comes into focus of the ways God has weaved His story of unfailing love.

Are you still waiting? Behind the scenes, out of human sight, our amazing God is doing amazing things. Keep your focus on Him, keep watch, and trust that His love is the best and He loves you the best. Someday soon, the wait will be over, and all will become clear in the light of God's glory and grace.

"I wait for the Lord, my soul does wait, and in His word do I hope. My soul waits for the Lord more than the watchmen for the morning; indeed, more than the watchmen for the morning." (Psalm 130:5-6, NASB)

"I have set the Lord continually before me; because He is at my right hand, I will not be shaken. Therefore, my heart is glad, and my glory rejoices; my flesh also will dwell securely." (Psalm 16:8-9, NASB

Wait and waiting

Word fun for those who wait...

Watchful
Anchored
In
Thanksgiving

Watching
Anticipating
Inclined
Toward
Indescribable
Next
Gift

Willing
All
In
Trust

"Meanwhile, friends, wait patiently for the Master's Arrival. You see farmers do this all the time, waiting for their valuable crops to mature, patiently letting the rain do its slow but sure work.

Be patient like that. Stay steady and strong. The Master could arrive at any time." (James 5:7-8, MSG)

The Light

Millions of stars shine in the heavens, their number beyond count, their brilliance beyond imagination. Unfortunately, the glaring lights of this world often blocks our sight of the heavenly lights. We can't see beyond the garish wattage of people's attempt to light their own way and walk in their own light.

The enemy tries to distract us from our bright, pure, and holy God. Satan wants us to focus on evil, and if he can't get us to focus on evil, he'll try to distract us with something that seems good to keep us from the best. Many are like cats chasing a tiny red dot instead of pursuing the everlasting light of Christ.

I know, I've been like a kitty chasing after any shiny object that came into my path. I've been distracted, blinded by the enemy, and often have missed the beauty and brilliance of God's best.

Oh, but how I want to step outside, outside of the rush, busyness, yelling, blaring and blinding of the world. Even if I can't escape physically, I can always escape spiritually. God's Word is a refuge, a place to still the soul and get the soul refocused on God's pure, bright and holy truth.

For years, the verse in Psalm 94:19 brought comfort. "When my anxious thoughts multiply within me, Your consolations delight my soul." To be honest, I read the verse wrong for decades, I thought it said constellations.

I thought the scripture was about getting outside and seeing the beauty of God's sky. Hey, it worked for me! ☺

No matter how distracting the world, the enemy, the busyness of life, God's light continues to shine. Walk in His light! Rejoice in His consolations and His constellations. Step away, step outside, turn your eyes to the heavens, for God's everlasting loving light always shines.

"When I consider Your heavens, the work of Your fingers, the moon and the stars, which You have ordained; what is man that You take thought of him, and the son of man that You care for him?" (Psalm 8:3-4, NASB)

"To Him who made the great lights, for His lovingkindness is everlasting: The sun to rule by day, for His lovingkindness is everlasting, the moon and stars to rule by night, for His lovingkindness is everlasting." (Psalm 136:7-9, NASB)

"Your word is a lamp to my feet and a light to my path." (Psalm 119:105, NASB)

Jesus said, "I am the light of the world. Anyone who follows Me will never walk in the darkness but will have the light of life." (John 8:12, HCSB)

Let the seed take root

During Bible study, prayer, listening to sermons and teachings, often there will be a jump in my spirit as a seed is planted by the Holy Spirit. I have a choice what will happen next. By meditating on The Word, watering with prayer and further Bible study, I allow the seed to take root. The harvest comes in my soul to plant and then share to bring forth a fruitful harvest.

I have a file on my computer with several hundred seeds, (verses, quotes, devotion ideas) small nuggets waiting for the time when they will be ready to go further. Sometimes the seed needs nurturing, time to grow, time to be fully realized. Other times, a seed may already be sprouting, ready to stand on its own and ready to be shared.

God, the Master Gardner, knows the correct timing for planting and for harvest. As we spend time with Him, He will show us the way to let the seeds take root.

What has the Holy Spirit been showing you? What seed has He planted in your heart? When a scripture and truth come to mind, write it down, ponder the truth, study God's word and apply it to your life.

Plant the seed by watering and nurturing through prayer and further study, then in the proper time share the seed and enjoy watching God's harvest blessings.

"As for what was sown on good soil, this is the one who hears the word and understands it. He indeed bears fruit and yields, in one case a hundredfold, in another sixty, and in another thirty." (Matthew 13:23, ESV)

Buffaloe scream

Ever needed a cleansing scream? You know like in the movies where the hero or heroine in utter agony lets out a primal yell? Years ago, after my husband's employer had shut down the facility where he worked, my sweet hubby had been searching for a new job for almost a full year. I was tired, so tired of waiting, and decided I really needed a deep, cathartic soul-cleansing.

Standing in the back yard, I called up all those nasty, desperate emotions from my very soul, took a deep breath, pulled in oxygen from several surrounding counties, opened my mouth and let a scream rip.

Unfortunately, my release sounded more like a bleating sheep—which caused my throat to freeze tight, the dogs in the neighborhood to start barking, squirrels to fall out of tree limbs, and an elderly neighbor to call animal control.

Bummer.

No relief and only a sore throat to show for my pitiful efforts, I tucked my proverbial tail and went back inside, up the stairs, into my office, plopped in my chair, and stared at my computer screen.

Finally, I did what I should have done in the first place – open my Bible. Sure enough, God was ready to listen regardless of my guttural scream ability.

As I read the Bible, verses provided the needed comfort. I'm so grateful God listens. Whether we think, whisper, scream, or bleat like sheep, God hears our cries.

The verses below cite references to our loving, attentive God. Whatever your need, and whatever method needed to talk to God, please take a moment to pray and talk to God.

"In my distress I called upon the Lord; I cried to my God, and He heard my voice from His temple; my cry came into His ears." (2 Samuel 22:7, AMP)

"Know that the LORD has set apart the godly for himself; the LORD will hear when I call to him." (Psalm 4:3, NIV)

"The LORD has heard my cry for mercy; the LORD accepts my prayer." (Psalm 6:9, NIV)

"Then you will call, and the LORD will answer; you will cry for help, and he will say: Here am I. ..." (Isaiah 58:9, NIV)

"Before they call I will answer; while they are still speaking I will hear." (Isaiah 65:24, NIV)

"This is the confidence we have in approaching God: that if we ask anything according to his will, he hears us. And if we know that he hears us— whatever we ask—we know that we have what we asked of him." (1 John 5:14-15, NIV)

"But I call to God, and the LORD saves me. Evening, morning and noon I cry out in distress, and he hears my voice." (Psalm 55:16-17, NIV)

"You are forgiving and good, O Lord, abounding in love to all who call to you." (Psalm 86:5, NIV)

"In the day of my trouble I will call to you, for you will answer me." (Psalm 86:7, NIV)

"He fulfills the desires of those who fear him; he hears their cry and saves them." (Psalm 145:19, NIV)

Nurturing the passion

Paul wrote to the Corinthians and the Ephesians regarding spiritual gifts. Each of us are equipped and gifted by the Holy Spirit for God's kingdom. Every single one of us is gifted in Christ. Wow and wahoo!

Unfortunately, in the turbulence of the world's difficulties, life becomes too busy, too hard, too painful, and many have allowed their giftings and passion to grow cold. Paul reminded Timothy to stir up, rekindle the embers, fan the flame, and keep burning the gracious gift of God -- the inner fire.

What we are given by God, we need to be diligent to be good servants and stewards of those gifts and blessings. Jesus said the greatest commandment is to love the Lord your God with all your heart, and with all your soul, and with all your mind.

When we love someone, we want to do things for them and spend time with them. Love prompts action and a desire to nurture that love. When we cherish our love of God, our love and passion will grow for God, and we will want to spend time with Him and please Him. What God gives us in gifts and blessings are to be used to gift and bless others, and when we do, we are blessed.

Heavenly Father, ignite in us a holy longing to spend time with You, to read Your word, and obey You. Open our eyes to see and our ears to hear so that we may closely follow You. Holy Spirit, blow on the coals of our hearts and reignite our passion to burn bright for You!

What gifts has God given you, what blessings have you received? Has your passion grown cold? Spend time with God and His word and let His holy fire rekindle the coals of your heart.

"Stir up (rekindle the embers of, fan the flame of, and keep burning) the [gracious] gift of God, [the inner fire] that is in you." (2 Timothy 1:6, AMPC)

Why I hate the news

The world tells us we need to be informed by watching or reading the news. Unfortunately, the news reports every murder, assault, and every negative and unpleasant situation around the world, then they interview argumentative, biased, offended people which creates and feeds fear, hopelessness, and argumentative, biased, offended people.

Satan must love the news because he wants people to be ineffective, fearful, bitter, scared, cowardly, hopeless, argumentative, biased, and offended.

We can stay informed, and we should be informed, but we do not have to saturate our minds with everything negative. Paul reminds us to think on what is true, honorable, right, pure, beautiful, and respected. Jesus tells us to seek first the kingdom of God.

We don't need to read the news to know the world is going up in flames, we need to read and bring the world to the Good News of the loving, purifying, holy flame of God.

If you want to be a better, more informed, smarter person, then fill your mind with things that eternally grow your mind. Feed your mind with the good word and the Word will feed you with God's best.

Dallas Willard reminds, "*We will fill our souls with the written Gospels. We will devote our attention to these teachings, in private study and inquiry as well as public instruction. And, negatively, we will refuse to devote our mental space and energy to the fruitless, even stupefying and degrading, stuff that constantly clamors for our attention. We will attend to it only enough to avoid it.*"[iii]

Jesus said to abide in Him (John 15:4) Abiding in Jesus (spending our time with Jesus, dwelling with Jesus) that is where we find peace, joy, fearlessness, hope, wisdom, and a fruitful life.

Therefore, "let's take a good look at the way we're living and reorder our lives under God." Remembering "bad company corrupts good morals." Therefore, "have nothing to do with the things done in darkness, which are not worth anything. But show that they are wrong. It is shameful even to talk about what those people do in secret. ... So be very careful how you live. Do not live like those who are not wise, but live wisely."

Finally, "brothers and sisters, think about the things that are good and worthy of praise. Think about the things that are true and honorable and right and pure and beautiful and respected. ... And the God who gives peace will be with you."

Lamentations 3:40, MSG), 1 Corinthians 15:33, NASB), Ephesians 5:11-15, NCV), Philippians 4:8-9, NCV)

The next minute

Have you ever thought, "I can't make it through another year, month, week, day, minute...?"

Please know God is there to help you through with enough grace, enough strength, enough mercy, and enough love.

God is with your every breath, every step, every need, and through everything, for the next year, month, week, day, minute, and second.

God's love is unfailing. He is with you every minute of every day. He will never leave you or forsake you. "The Lord is a stronghold for the oppressed, a stronghold in times of trouble." (Psalm 9:9, ESV)

"For in the time of trouble He shall hide me in His pavilion; in the secret place of His tabernacle, He shall hide me; He shall set me high upon a rock." (Psalm 27:5, NKJV)

"Therefore, let everyone who is faithful pray to You at a time that You may be found. When great floodwaters come, they will not reach him. You are my hiding place; You protect me from trouble. You surround me with joyful shouts of deliverance." (Psalm 32:6-7, HCSB)

Every minute, God is in the minute with you. "Trust in Him at all times, O people..." (Psalm 62:8, NASB)

Relaxing in His hands

Have you ever been in a body of water completely panicked, with arms flailing, thinking you're drowning, when in reality all you had to do was lower your feet and stand? I've been there, done that. Rather embarrassing, but very comforting when those toes touch sand or terra firma.

How often as Christians do we flounder, flap, and flail in the midst of our circumstances? (I'll be honest, I can flounder, flap, and flail with the rest).

How often do we forget that Jesus's promise that no one can snatch us out of His hands or the hands of God the Father? Stop, rest, think about, and relish that wonderful truth. When we take the time to be still, and know that God is God, remembering He is in control and we are loved, our flailing stops.

God tells us to cease striving, be still, and know that He is God. "Be still" in Hebrew means to sink down, let drop, be quiet, or relax.

When rescuing a drowning victim, Lifeguards need the person to be still, to stop flailing and trust the skills of the lifeguard. The calmer the person, the easier the rescue.

Fortunately, even in the crashing waves of problems and difficulties, even when we are flailing and panicked, we can lean back, confident in the palm of God's Hands.

No matter what difficulties you face, you really are always safe in God's hands. You are forever firmly planted in His love.

The Hands which formed you and gave you life, beckons you to relax in the life of His loving hands. You are always held secure in the Hands of Jesus.

Relax and remember you are lovingly held by God. No matter where you are, or what is happening, God's hands will never let you fall.

"I give them eternal life, and they will never perish, and no one will snatch them out of my hand. My Father, who has given them to me, is greater than all, and no one is able to snatch them out of the Father's hand." (John 10:28-29, ESV)

Anointed to...

As Jesus' ministry began, He stood in the temple and read from Isaiah, "The Spirit of the Lord is upon Me, because He anointed Me to preach the gospel to the poor. He has sent Me to proclaim release to the captives, and recovery of sight to the blind, to set free those who are oppressed, to proclaim the favorable year of the Lord" (Luke 4:18-19).

When I read these verses, there is a jump in my spirit, because the words that Jesus shared are a call for us as Christ followers. When we become Christians, Jesus comes and lives in our hearts. Therefore, the anointing Jesus received is passed on to us to preach the gospel, to proclaim release to those held captive by sin, recovery of sight to those blinded by the enemy, and to point others to Christ who sets free those who are oppressed.

As Christ followers, we have a calling and an anointing. Peter tells us we are a royal priesthood to proclaim the excellencies of God who called us out of darkness into light. Through Christ, we are anointed to light the world with His light. Oh, the thrill of being a Christian!

Jesus tells us "anyone who believes in me will do the same works I have done, and even greater works." Wow! The Spirit of the living God breathes His life within us to share His life with a lost world. We are anointed and unlimited by our limitless God.

You have a beautiful, wonderful, anointed calling. Therefore, tell others about Christ and shine His light!

"The Spirit of the Lord God is upon me, because the Lord has anointed me to bring good news to the afflicted; He has sent me to bind up the brokenhearted, to proclaim liberty to captives and freedom to prisoners; to proclaim the favorable year of the Lord and the day of vengeance of our God; to comfort all who mourn, to grant those who mourn in Zion, giving them a garland instead of ashes, The oil of gladness instead of mourning, the mantle of praise instead of a spirit of fainting. So, they will be called oaks of righteousness, the planting of the Lord, that He may be glorified." (Isaiah 61:1-3, NASB)

"...you are a chosen race, a royal priesthood, a holy nation, a people for God's own possession, so that you may proclaim the excellencies of Him who has called you out of darkness into His marvelous light." (1 Peter 2:9, NASB)

"You are the light of the world. A city set on a hill cannot be hidden; nor does anyone light a lamp and put it under a basket, but on the lampstand, and it gives light to all who are in the house." (Matthew 5:14-15, NASB)

"I tell you the truth, anyone who believes in me will do the same works I have done, and even greater works, because I am going to be with the Father." (John 14:12, NLT)

Heart cry

Have you ever been desperate to know if you pleased God? I have. Even though I can recite verses on God's love and know God loves His children, there are times I wonder if I'm doing what He has called me to do.

The other day, fighting back tears, troubled deep in my heart, I sat in my chair. In my soul, I cried out to God asking Him if I pleased Him. Before I could even finish the heart cry, I received a sweet message from a friend. Then, at Bible study God blessed with another encouragement when I learned the church library was going to carry all my books. Then, a young woman in our Bible study group bought me lunch. Then, another woman in our group gave me her winning ticket to win a book and audio tape. Then the next day, I received an email from a Christian organization who ran my article in their magazine and now want to use it for a Gospel tract. The blessings came and came and came.

Those sweet blessings don't happen every day and were definitely gifts beyond measure. Most days I plug along in silence wondering if anyone notices or cares and if what I do matters.

We all need assurance and encouragement. However, the truth is, whether we see with our eyes or feel with our emotions, or hear with our ears, we can be assured God's love is constant.

God loves you on your good days and your bad days. He **is** love, so therefore, His love never changes.

Is your heart troubled? Dear friend, God loves you and His ears are attentive to His children. Cry out to Him, listen and watch, and regardless of what you see or feel, remember His love is constant and unchanging.

"**L**et my [mournful] cry come before You, O Lord; give me understanding [the ability to learn and a teachable heart] according to Your word [of promise]." (Psalm 119:169, AMP)

"I love the Lord, because He hears [and continues to hear] My voice and my supplications (my pleas, my cries, my specific needs)." (Psalm 116:1, AMP)

"Hear the voice of my supplication (specific requests, humble entreaties) as I cry to You for help, as I lift up my hands and heart toward Your innermost sanctuary (Holy of Holies)." (Psalm 28:2, AMP)

"Peace I leave with you; My [perfect] peace I give to you; not as the world gives do I give to you. Do not let your heart be troubled, nor let it be afraid. [Let My perfect peace calm you in every circumstance and give you courage and strength for every challenge.]" (John 14:27, AMP)

Squished

Have you ever had one of those days you feel life is squishing the stuffing out of you? David asked God to search his heart and thoughts to see if there was anything grievous within him (Psalm 139:23-24). Some versions read "investigate, cross-examine, try me," and it also means to check what pops out under pressure.

Since most of us don't live cloistered on some mountaintop, it's hard to keep emotions and thoughts on an even keel when we are squashed by hardships and difficulties. Real life = real problems. Sometimes stuff hits on the blindside, and **boom**, out pops something improper. Yikes! What is stored up bursts out under strain.

I have a better chance of reacting properly to life if I spend time with God – whether reading the Bible, working on Bible study, and/or listening to praise music. Sit me by the river with praise music playing, and an atomic bomb might not rattle me. Ah, bliss!

The Psalmist said he hid God's word in his heart so he wouldn't sin against God. Paul reminds us to think about things that are good and worthy of praise, true and honorable, right, pure, and beautiful and respected (Philippians 4:8).

Therefore, to avoid unpleasant stuff squishing out, make sure to saturate with God's word and the good God has created. Let's feed in with God's good and the good is what will squish out.

Are you feeling squished by problems and difficulties? Spend time with God, read the Bible and allow His word in to saturate and cover your mind to protect against anything negative squishing out.

"I have stored up your word in my heart, that I might not sin against you." (Psalm 119:11, ESV)

The gaping hole

My heart broke for the heartache of my friends -- loved ones had been lost, some quickly in tragic ways, others had watched their family members slip away slowly through illness. All my friends were left with a deep hole in their hearts no person can fill.

Tragedies, death, and life changes can leave us reeling and wondering how we will ever again find our footing. With an ending, our plans, hopes, and dreams are upended, and we can't fathom how things will again feel right and how to move on without those we love.

Would you join me in prayer?

Oh Father, in Your unfailing love and mercy please fill the gaping hole in our lives and our friend's lives. Oh, how our loved ones are missed. God of all comfort, please comfort with Your comfort. Thank You for Your tender love, please shower them with Your peace and the knowledge that You are always with them.

Please cover their minds and hearts from the lies of the enemy during this vulnerable time. Though they walk through the valley of the shadow of death, You are with them. Every tear they cry is precious to You, none fall without Your loving hand to catch, hold, and cherish. Oh Father, it is so hard to lose our loved ones. Prince of Peace, please shelter them in Your peace.

Heavenly Father, please grant my friends time to grieve with You. Hide them in the shadow of Your wings. Thank You that You understand the cries and groans of their wounded hearts. Thank You their breaking hearts are always safe in You, for You are the God who turns evil into good for those who love You. You provide grace, mercy, comfort, and strength for every heartbreaking moment.

Oh Father, please, please, please, fill the gaping hole in their hearts with Your unfailing hope and love. You are the One who made their hearts, You know how deep the wounds, fill them with You, Father. Fill them to the brim with Your love. Hold them close as they grieve, hold them through the dark valley until they again can feel the warmth of Your Sonshine.

Thank You that one day You will wipe every tear from their eyes and there will be no more death, mourning, crying, or pain. Until then Father, please fill the gaping hole in their hearts with Your love.

"The righteous cry, and the Lord hears and delivers them out of all their troubles. The Lord is near to the brokenhearted and saves those who are crushed in spirit. Many are the afflictions of the righteous, but the Lord delivers him out of them all. The Spirit also helps our weakness; for we do not know how to pray as we should, but the Spirit Himself intercedes for us with groanings too deep for words. He heals the brokenhearted and binds up their wounds and He will wipe away every tear from their eyes; and there will no longer be any death; there will no longer be any mourning, or crying, or pain." (Psalm 34:17-19, NASB), Romans 8:26, NASB). Psalm 147:3, NKJV), Revelation 21:4, NASB)

The sounds

The fall afternoon beckoned, and a friend and I visited a local park to enjoy the beautiful weather. Birds happily chirped as a slight breeze played among the red, yellow, and brown trees lining the paved path. Deep in conversation we barely noticed our surroundings ... until the winding trail became covered in dark shadows.

My friend joked about a scene from a scary movie and the now-quiet woods no longer looked friendly. A gentle rustling in the leaves, made us pause and glance up to the tree-lined hill next to us. Seeing nothing, we picked up the pace. The rustling turned to crashing, with the sound of someone, or something, in pursuit. In an all-out panic, we raced to reach the car.

Safe inside the locked automobile, we laughed and wondered what had made the sound. Even if it had been a small animal running through the leaves, we were wise to take precautions.

Sounds can cause a myriad of emotions and reactions. Filmmakers use musical scores to build the mood and audience response they desire. Be careful what you hear, who you listen to, and what sounds get your attention. Satan is devious, a wolf in sheep's clothing, tickling ears with the sounds of his lies to manipulate and deceive.

In the bombardment of noise in this world, God's voice, His Word is The Truth. By reading scripture out loud, listening to praise music, praising God, and talking of the truth in scripture, our souls are calmed, quieted, and lifted in rejoicing and worship.

Focus on God's promises, His eternal security, and His unfailing love, those truths will lift you high above the sounds of the world and the noise of the enemy. Speak, sing, and praise God, and you'll find restoration and rejoicing for your heart and soul.

"Sing to him, sing praises to him; tell of all his wondrous works! Glory in his holy name; let the hearts of those who seek the Lord rejoice!" (1 Chronicles 16:9-10, ESV)

Crazy times

We live in crazy times. Common sense, hard-work, and Christian ethics seem to have flown out the window and crashed to the ground. People are angry about all sorts of things, and I don't think many are really sure why they are so angry. False reports, fake news, slander, and innuendo is commonplace in every form of media. It's nasty out there!

Satan wants to silence, shame, and keep Christians afraid and fearful. The devil is an accuser, a liar who is out to steal, kill, and destroy. Godly people are persecuted and attacked. While we are on this earth, we will have battles. Hunkering down and hiding doesn't make us victorious or grant victory.

If we remember who we are in Christ, the power we have in Christ, the inheritance in Christ, a glorious, wonderful, unending, beautiful inheritance, we would stand tall and stand firm. We are here, now, in these crazy times for an amazing purpose. We are not left defenseless.

I picture myself standing in front of an angry mob, my knees are knocking, and I want to run and hide. But then, the crowd is silenced, their eyes grow wide with fear. Not because of me, but **He** who is inside of me and stands with me. God has given His power through Christ to fight every battle. I don't have to be brave and strong to fight; my help comes from the Lord who made heaven and earth.

Satan is getting louder, but his volume has no effect on our all-powerful God.

Our God who is greater than all, lives within us. Nothing, and no one, can stand against our God. The enemy roars, but our Savior is THE LION!

Be strong in the power of Christ. Speak truth. Live in love. Your future is secure and no one, not anyone, can ever take away your eternal security. You are a child of the King, are given His wisdom, and everything you need for these crazy times. Stand firm. "Say to those with fearful hearts, 'Be strong, do not fear; your God will come, he will come with vengeance; with divine retribution he will come to save you.'" (Isaiah 35:4, NIV)

"For God did not give us a spirit of timidity or cowardice or fear, but [He has given us a spirit] of power and of love and of sound judgment and personal discipline [abilities that result in a calm, well-balanced mind and self-control]. So do not be ashamed to testify about our Lord ... continue to preach regardless of the circumstances, in accordance with the power of God for His power is invincible (2 Timothy 1:7-8, AMP)

"Do not be agitated by evildoers; do not envy those who do wrong. For they wither quickly like grass and wilt like tender green plants. Trust in the Lord and do what is good; dwell in the land and live securely. Take delight in the Lord, and He will give you your heart's desires. Commit your way to the Lord; rust in Him, and He will act, making your righteousness shine like the dawn, your justice like the noonday. Be silent before the Lord and wait expectantly for Him; do not be agitated by one who prospers in his way, by the man who carries out evil plans. Refrain from anger and give up your rage; do not be agitated—it can only bring harm. For evildoers will be destroyed, but those who put their hope in the Lord will inherit the land. A little while, and the wicked person will be no more; though you look for him, he will not be there. But the humble will inherit the land and will enjoy abundant prosperity." (Psalm 37:1-11, HCSB)

"Be sober [well balanced and self-disciplined], be alert and cautious at all times. That enemy of yours, the devil, prowls around like a roaring lion [fiercely hungry], seeking someone to devour." (1 Peter 5:8, AMP)

"We are human, but we don't wage war as humans do. We use God's mighty weapons, not worldly weapons, to knock down the strongholds of human reasoning and to destroy false arguments. We destroy every proud obstacle that keeps people from knowing God. We capture their rebellious thoughts and teach them to obey Christ. For we are not fighting against flesh-and-blood enemies, but against evil rulers and authorities of the unseen world, against mighty powers in this dark world, and against evil spirits in the heavenly places." ~2 Corinthians 10:3-5, NLT), Ephesians 6:12, NLT)

Tomorrow

Poor Tomorrow is viewed as a friend or a foe. If we're excited about what is coming, we can't wait for tomorrow. Yay, for tomorrow. Tomorrow is such a wonderful day!

However, if something negative is in the near future, or we think something is going to be negative, poor tomorrow is not talked about in positive terms.

Jesus said to not worry about tomorrow or be anxious for tomorrow, that it will care for itself (Matthew 6:34). James reminds us we don't have a clue about what will happen tomorrow (James 4:14).

So, I've been wondering about tomorrow, because when I wake tomorrow, tomorrow will be today, so does tomorrow really exist? And why should I worry about something that doesn't exist? No wonder tomorrow will care for itself, it kind of vanishes in the light of today. Tomorrow is just a date that doesn't have a date.

Our God is so good, mighty, and wonderful. We don't have to worry about tomorrow because our God is timeless. Give your tomorrow to God. No need to worry, God is here today, He is already in tomorrow, and when you wake in the morning, He will be with you today.

"Trust in him at all times, O people; pour out your heart before him; God is a refuge for us. Selah" (Psalm 62:8, NIV)

Expecting the best

During a time of prayer, I wondered, what if I expected the best from God? What if I expected the best, because God's ways are the best, His love is the best, and He loves me the best?

I've been reading books by people who are currently living in countries where Christians are persecuted. These people have amazing faith and witness many miracles. I wonder is that because they have no pre-conceived notions about what God can and cannot do? They expect God to move in mighty ways and therefore see Him move in mighty ways.

In many areas, religion is boxed into a sanitized version of Christianity. "Now He did not do many mighty works there because of their unbelief." (Matthew 13:58, NKJV)

If we never expect the best, will we ever see the best?

"God baptizes us with holy boldness and divine confidence for He is looking not for great people but for people who will dare to prove the greatness of their God!" ~ A. B. Simpson

"In your prayers, above everything else, beware of limiting God, not only through unbelief but also by thinking you know exactly what He can do. Learn to expect the unexpected, beyond all that you ask or think." ~ Andrew Murray

What if I lived in the holy boldness and divine confidence by remembering the greatness of my God? What if I expected the unexpected of exceedingly, abundantly more than I could ask or imagine? Just writing those words, I can feel a holy confidence rising within me.

The Truth is that nothing is impossible for God. His love is unfailing, His supremacy is unstoppable, and His might is mightier than anything or anyone.

As Christians, His power lives within us. The best, The Very Best, lives within us. Does my life, and do my prayers, change when I remember those facts? To be honest, yes. Problems become smaller when I view situations through the lens of our great God. Dreams become bigger when I remember the might and power of our GREAT God.

Worry and hesitation ends as boldness and confidence takes over because my boldness and confidence rests in our loving, unfailing, ALL-POWERFUL God.

Heavenly Father, I want Your best and Your perfect will. Through the hard, difficult, good, bad, and ugly, please grant me eyes to watch for how You are moving and working. Help me live in Your holy boldness and confidence. I want to see and experience the exceedingly, abundantly more than I could ask or imagine. Nothing is too hard for You, nothing is impossible for You, for You are a GREAT God! Help me never limit You and always expect the best, for You are the BEST! Praise You Holy Father! I love You! I ask these things in the name of Your Son, Jesus Christ, who is my Savior. Amen!

Restless

I gazed at the photograph of the Japanese woman in traditional dress. Her face serene, body relaxed and calm, she sat facing a well-tended garden. I envied her. How did she have such a look of tranquility?

As a Christian, I know I should be peaceful. Psalm 46:10 tells us to "cease striving" and know that He is God. Oh, I wanted to cease striving, but for several months (what seemed like decades), I had been out of rest, restless, troubled, keyed-up, wound-up, agitated, edgy, restless, restless, restless, and more restless.

Serene and calm seemed out of reach. Not understanding what kept me wound tight, I prayed and begged God, desperate for Him to wrestle the restlessness out of me. I discovered some of the issues came from a vitamin deficiency and hormone changes, and God graciously showed a few areas that needed His truth.

Yet, something remained that continued to irritate. God is not a God of confusion but of peace, so what was bringing this restless confusion? Then it hit me, I live in enemy territory. Satan is out to steal, kill, and destroy. Peter warned us the devil prowls around like a roaring lion seeking someone to devour. Paul said to put on the full armor of God so we can stand against the schemes of the devil and the spiritual forces of darkness.

Our struggle isn't against flesh and blood.
That's it!

Most of my restless, internal struggle was coming from external forces. I had forgotten the enemy and let down my guard. I needed to draw my sword of the Spirit to use against Satan and his schemes.

Jesus said the truth will set us free, and His truth is the key to freedom. When confused about something, restless about something, run to God and seek His wisdom. Nothing that troubles you is greater than God. No scheme of the enemy is greater than God. Put on your armor, take up your shield of faith, use your sword of the Spirit, and stand firm on the truth of His word.

"...God is not a God of confusion but of peace..." (1 Corinthians 14:33, NASB)

"Be of sober spirit, be on the alert. Your adversary the devil, prowls around like a roaring lion, seeking someone to devour." (1 Peter 5:8, NASB)

"Put on the full armor of God, so that you will be able to stand firm against the schemes of the devil. For our struggle is not against flesh and blood, but against the rulers, against the powers, against the world forces of this darkness, against the spiritual forces of wickedness in the heavenly places. Therefore, take up the full armor of God, so that you will be able to resist in the evil day, and having done everything, to stand firm. Stand firm therefore, having girded your loins with truth, and having put on the breastplate of righteousness, and having shod your feet with the preparation of the gospel of peace; in addition to all, taking up the shield of faith with which you will be able to extinguish all the flaming arrows of the evil one. And take the helmet of salvation, and the sword of the Spirit, which is the word of God." (Ephesians 6:11-17, NASB)

"...He who is in you is greater than he who is in the world." (1 John 4:4, NASB)

"Let be and be still and know (recognize and understand) that I am God. I will be exalted among the nations! I will be exalted in the earth! The Lord of hosts is with us; the God of Jacob is our Refuge (our High Tower and Stronghold). Selah [pause, and calmly think of that]!" (Psalm 46:10-11, AMPC)

Untangled

Ever had your stomach tangled in knots? The stress of the day, of the news, of the world, can wreak havoc on the body. Whew, it's a crazy world out there, people.

All too often I get tangled up in the messiness of the messy world. Paul's advice to Timothy made me wonder how to get untangled.

Here are a few ideas...

Spend more time in Bible study and prayer. Focus back on the might of our ALL-MIGHTY God. Remember God is our defender, and we don't battle with flesh and blood. Through Christ we are given His power and His strength for any and every battle. God's heavenly forces are bigger than any earthly or demonic forces. There is nothing impossible with God and He is ALL-powerful.

Limit the stream of negative news. Turn off the Television, step away from the online social scene, and don't get dragged down by reading (or watching) everyone else's opinions or thoughts. Seek first God's kingdom and His righteousness (Matthew 6:33).

Remember, we can't fix the world, but through prayer can carry the world to The One who can fix everything. We are not left defenseless. We are never defenseless when we have Christ Jesus in our lives.

Stay on task to do what the Lord has called us to do in the various aspects of our lives. Work to please God, not to please men.

Pray. Pray. Pray. Prayer accesses the power of all-mighty God. When seeing something troubling, take those troubles to God and pray mighty prayers. On our knees, we can change this world.

Finally, live untangled in the freedom of Christ by keeping the focus on our Master and live to please Him.

"No soldier gets entangled in civilian pursuits, since his aim is to please the one who enlisted him." (2 Timothy 2:4, ESV)

A Christmas message for every day of the year

Christmas isn't about money or gifts. Christmas is personal. Christmas is love. The Creator came to save creation. Boundless became bound. Glory became flesh. The embodiment of love wrapped in the soft, smooth skin of an infant. A wooden manger cradles the cradle of Life. A feeding trough for the Bread of Heaven.

The Great Shepherd's arrival announced to those who tended sheep to call to the lost sheep. Jesus Christ, the Bread of Heaven, born to feed a soul-starved, hungry, and dying world. Jesus Christ, Immanuel, God with us, born to bring joy midst chaos, suffering, and the pain of life. Jesus Christ, Savior, born to love, sacrifice, and save.

Jesus Christ, our hope, born to bring hope to the hopeless. Birthed to die to grant us living hope through His resurrection, and through Him new life is birthed in us. Jesus Christ, the Peace. Yet peace that came to bring a sword—the sword of the Spirit to slash through our earthly confines and released us to true freedom in Christ.

Jesus Christ, The Word, speaks the words that bring life. Jesus came to live in our hearts. Hearts broken and damaged. Hearts now restored and renewed by His touch. Christmas (and every day) is a reminder that God loves you.

Regardless of what exists in your past, present, or future, God is with you. You are never alone, you are guaranteed hope, and forever loved.

Jesus gave Himself and offers total connection, uninterrupted opportunities to be in His presence. We are the ones who hinder the flow, busy doing and living and being that we miss the baby in the manger. The one who brought humanity the gift of Himself so that we may live eternally through Him.

For there has been born for you a Savior, who is Christ the Lord. He Who gifted life, gifts again with abundant, eternal life through the nail-scarred hands of Jesus.

Will you hurry to your Savior? Will you spread the word? As the star drew the magi to Bethlehem will our lives draw others to Christ?

Oh, what can I bring to The King? What can I give You my King? What do I have to offer to The One who created all? Without Jesus, I would have been lost forever. Without hope. Without redemption. Without love. Without The life that gave me life.

Words that I write and speak, life that I live, all are only a speck in the cosmos. I long to bring You— My King, My Creator, my life, my all—something that will make Your heart smile.

What can I bring The King? The only thing that no one else can bring... Me.

What will you gift the King? Will you give The King, your ear, your focus, your heart, your dreams, your passions, your life, your all? This Christmas, and every day of the year, will you gift The King the only thing no one else can bring? *You.*

Next time

Desperate to be free, I fought and screamed. Awakened by my cries, my sweet husband gently shook me awake. I had been trapped in a dream, ensnared by demon arms, imprisoned, and couldn't escape. Three times that night the enemy attacked. I escaped the first two nightmares but couldn't seem to escape the last on my own. Finally free, I shuddered in the night, pressed tight in my strong husband's arms.

Satan whispered, taunted, hissed, *"Next time you will be alone. Next time you won't get away."*

The devil is a liar. He preys on vulnerable moments, kicks while we are down, then screeches his lies in our ears, minds, and nightmares. **The truth is, we are never alone. No matter what happens next time, God is always in that time.** And if you have messed up "that" time or "this" time, remember God is God for all times. **God makes all things new.**

God redeems **all** time. He is a stronghold, strong tower, rescuer, redeemer, and restorer. He is always with you. God will never leave or forsake you. Jesus Christ saves for all eternity, and for all time you are forever free in His love.

No weapon, no demonic attack, no nightmare, no matter what happens **next time**, our times are in the hands of our all-mighty God.

Heavenly Father, help me to stand firm on the truth that Your unfailing love surrounds me. Father, You will keep me safe against all enemy attacks.

The battles may rage, but You are always with me and You have won the final war. Thank You that You make all things new, and Your mercies are new every morning. Keep my mind clearly focused on You. In all times, help me to trust and rest in You knowing I am safe and sound forever in Your love.

"...**I trust in you, Lord; I say, 'You are my God.' My times are in your hands**; deliver me from the hands of my enemies, from those who pursue me. Let your face shine on your servant; save me in your unfailing love." (Psalm 31:14-16, NIV)

"Though I walk in the midst of trouble, You will revive me; You will stretch forth Your hand against the wrath of my enemies, And Your right hand will save me. The Lord will accomplish what concerns me; Your lovingkindness, O Lord, is everlasting.... Psalm 138:7-8, NASB)

"The Lord also will be a stronghold for the oppressed, a stronghold in times of trouble." (Psalm 9:9, NASB)

"Dear friend, guard clear thinking and common sense with your life; don't for a minute lose sight of them. They'll keep your soul alive and well, they'll keep you fit and attractive. You'll travel safely, you'll neither tire nor trip. You'll take afternoon naps without a worry; **you'll enjoy a good night's sleep. No need to panic over alarms or surprises, or predictions that doomsday's just around the corner, because God will be right there with you; he'll keep you safe and sound.**" ~Proverbs 3:21-26, MSG) (emphasis added on scripture)

Rollerblading Christianity

When I think of friendships, I imagine we're all skating through life on roller blades. Some people with wobbly legs cling on the outskirts holding to the wall, others sit on the floor too unsure to move. There are those who skate with confidence, and in the center of the rink are the gifted ones who pirouette, leap, and frolic with ease.

As friends, brothers and sisters in Christ, we can help one another. Those who are afraid are encouraged by those with more confidence. Fearful floor dwellers are uplifted, shaky legs steadied. Stronger ones provide stability, teaching proper techniques. Then, when the weaker one gains strength, they slingshot off and zoom past as their friend's cheer their success. That person then helps another, and on and on it goes, until we all skate into Heaven with the people we've met along our journey.

I laugh quite often with one of my sweet friends, Teena, about this visual. As I've traveled around the country with various moves, we've watched as God has led us through trials, heartaches, and joyful adventures. One moment she slingshots past me with an amazing opportunity to serve the Lord, and then another year, God opens a door for me. It's been a grand adventure. We joke that even with our short hair styles, our pigtails are flying in the Holy Spirit wind.

You too have a place. Someone needs your hand, needs that extra help in the roller-rink of life.

Others are here for you, holding on when you need a little assistance. In the stands, are ones cheering from the sideline and praying.

I (and others) need you in the rink of life. Your friendship, prayers, your hands, help, and encouragement, they are all needed. Link hands and link shields of faith, because you are needed, and let those pig-tails fly!

"Two are better than one because they have a good return for their labor. For if either of them falls, the one will lift up his companion. But woe to the one who falls when there is not another to lift him up." (Ecclesiastes 4:9-10, NASB)

"A friend loves at all times, and a brother is born for adversity." (Proverbs 17:17, NASB)

"Therefore encourage one another and build up one another, just as you also are doing." (1 Thessalonians 5:11, NASB)

Stability in the instability

No matter how unstable our environment, politics, the world, your current situation, or whatever the future may hold, God is everlasting stability. He is the solid rock, our firm foundation. He is the eternal loving Father, unfailing, immovable, and unchangeable.

Your world may be shaking, but HE who is above the world is always stable. His hold on you, on your precious soul, is always firm and always loving. "He is your constant source of stability; he abundantly provides safety and great wisdom; he gives all this to those who fear him." (Isaiah 33:6, NET Bible)

"Do not fear, for I am with you; do not be afraid, for I am your God. I will strengthen you; I will help you; I will hold on to you with My righteous right hand. For I, Yahweh your God, hold your right hand and say to you: Do not fear, I will help you." (Isaiah 41:10, Isaiah 41:13, HCSB)

"I love you, Lord. You are my strength. The Lord is my rock, my protection, my Savior. My God is my rock. I can run to him for safety. He is my shield and my saving strength, my defender. I will call to the Lord, who is worthy of praise, and I will be saved from my enemies." (Psalm 18:1-3, NCV)

"He alone is my rock and my salvation, my stronghold; I will not be shaken." (Psalm 62:6, HCSB)

You are...

The enemy plants untruths because of what happened, where you were raised, your heritage, your upbringing, your mistakes, that you are a failure, unloved, worthless, a mistake, not worthy, unredeemable, hopeless. Don't believe the lies of Satan, especially since the enemy is behind all those negative things in your life and in the world.

The truth is not found in what you are, what you were, or what you will be, the truth is found in the great I AM. God, The I AM, says because of your relationship with Jesus you are forgiven and free, a child of the King.

As a Christian, your identity never changes and is never altered by the past, present, or future. Regardless of what happened or what may happen, you are a child of the Great I AM.

Blow out the lies of the enemy and breathe in deep the truth of who you are in Christ. You are loved by your heavenly Father, The King. The truth is, you are secure in God's hand, and are always and forever His beloved child.

"when the right time came, God sent his Son, born of a woman, subject to the law. God sent him to buy freedom for us who were slaves to the law, so that he could adopt us as his very own children. And because we are his children, God has sent the Spirit of his Son into our hearts, prompting us to call out, 'Abba, Father.' Now you are no longer a slave but God's own child. And since you are his child, God has made you his heir." (Galatians 4:4-7, NLT)

"He gave the right and the power to become children of God to those who received Him. He gave this to those who put their trust in His name." (John 1:12 (NLV)

"What marvelous love the Father has extended to us! Just look at it—we're called children of God! That's who we really are...." (1 John 3:1, MSG)

Keep Going!

Problems come and difficulties arise. Life can be a maze of frustrations. Persistence is key for each obstacle giving opportunity for growth and maturity. Remember, whatever God has called you to do, He will be with you to supply all your needs to equip you for your journey. Keep going!

Run the race. "Do you not know that those who run in a race all run, but only one receives the prize? Run in such a way that you may win." (1 Corinthians 9:24, NASB)

Remember God will "equip you with everything good for doing his will, and may he work in us what is pleasing to him, through Jesus Christ, to whom be glory forever and ever. Amen. (Hebrews 13:20-21, NIV)

God "will supply all your needs according to His riches in glory in Christ Jesus." (Philippians 4:19, NASB)

Keep working. "Jesus replied, 'No one who puts his hand to the plow and looks back is fit for service in the kingdom of God.' (Luke 9:62, NIV)

Keep at the work you've been called to do. "Be diligent in these matters; give yourself wholly to them, so that everyone may see your progress. Be diligent to present yourself approved to God as a workman who does not need to be ashamed, accurately handling the word of truth."." ~1 Timothy 4:15, NIV), 2 Timothy 2:15, NASB)

Give your desires to God. "I delight to do Your will, O my God; Your Law is within my heart." (Psalm 40:8, NASB)

Whatever you do, do for God's glory. "Not to us, O Lord, not to us, but to Your name give glory because of Your lovingkindness, because of Your truth." (Psalm 115:1, NASB)

Give yourself freely to God. "With a freewill offering I will sacrifice to you; I will give thanks to your name, O Lord, for it is good." (Psalm 54:6, ESV)

Delight in God. "Delight yourself in the Lord; and He will give you the desires of your heart." (Psalm 37, NASB)

Abound in every good work. "Grow in the grace and knowledge of our Lord and Savior Jesus Christ. To Him be the glory, both now and to the day of eternity. Amen." (2 Peter 3:18, NASB)

Keep fighting the good fight. "Fight the good fight of faith; take hold of the eternal life to which you were called, and you made the good confession in the presence of many witnesses." (1 Timothy 6:12, NASB)

Keep zealous in your work for the Lord. "Never be lacking in zeal, but keep your spiritual fervor, serving the Lord. Be joyful in hope, patient in affliction, faithful in prayer." (Romans 12:11-12, NIV)

God is faithful to complete what He starts. Be "confident of this, that he who began a good work in you will carry it on to completion until the day of Christ Jesus." (Philippians 1:6, NIV)

Keep going, don't give up, don't slack off, and don't let the enemy deter your walk in the Lord.

Nothing is impossible for God and there is no power, person, or situation bigger than God. Keep your focus on Christ and remember His promises, and remember He is always with you for now and through eternity. Keep going!

"Be brave. Be strong. Don't give up." (Psalm 31:23a, MSG)

When the enemy comes like a flood

At four a.m., from a sound sleep, I heard in my spirit, "*Open your eyes*." In the darkness of our room, I could see a black cloud moving toward my side of the bed, toward me.

I had no fear, just watched, then the Lord spoke in my soul...*The enemy will come like a flood. Resist. Stand firm. I will be with you.*

As I prayed, pondered and listened, more was given during those early morning hours. Some of the prayer time is personal, but other things I think will be helpful for more than just me. At first, I wasn't sure if I should share the long list of Bible verses, but so many friends mentioned they too are in the midst of a battle and in need of prayer and scripture help.

The verses I found are in relation to the hours I spent with the Lord. Some of the things He spoke into my spirit, I believe apply to us all.

Nothing is impossible. Be strong (in God's strength). *I will be with you. Nothing is impossible for God. The enemy means to destroy you, I will use it to free you. To set you free.* (I thought of Shadrach, Meshach, and Abednego. They were thrown in the blazing fire, but nothing was burnt off them except the ropes that bound them.)

Hold on to Me. No fear. Do not be afraid. Do not worry or let your heart be troubled. I will give you treasures in the darkness. Peace like a river. Stay in My Word. The truth will set you free.

Battle plan –
#1 Stay close to God.
#2 Stay in His Word. His truth will set us free.

Whatever battle you face, the Lord has given you His words to help you get through and be victorious. Make notes, spend time with God, write out what you are facing, pray and ask God for His truth to help you. Use your Bible, and if you have the internet (or smart phone), use Bible applications to search based on word or phrases. God's truth will feed your soul and will set you free.

The verses you find on the next pages are ones I found for my specific battle. God's Word is a light to our path, and whatever darkness we face, His light will shine to give us guidance, help, and wisdom.

As you read through, prayerfully ask the Lord to highlight Bible verses that will help you in your journey. God never leaves us alone to fight our battles, and He is all-powerful for our every need.

For my battle, the first scriptures that came to mind pertains to the Israelites sending out their praise and worship team before them and God routing the enemy. "When they began singing and praising, the Lord set ambushes against the sons of Ammon, Moab and Mount Seir, who had come against Judah; so they were routed." (2 Chronicles 20:22, NASB) Therefore, I will praise the Lord and watch the Lord rout the enemy!

Remember always, we are safe forever in God's mighty, All-powerful hand.

"I give them eternal life, and they shall never perish; no one will snatch them out of my hand. My Father, who has given them to me, is greater than all; no one can snatch them out of my Father's hand. I and the Father are one." (John 10:28-30, NIV)

God and His Word gives us stability. "Everyone who comes to Me and hears My words and acts on them, I will show you whom he is like: he is like a man building a house, who dug deep and laid a foundation on the rock; and when a flood occurred, the torrent burst against that house and could not shake it, because it had been well built." (Luke 6:47-48, NASB)

Submission to God and resistance against the devil, gives us freedom. "Submit therefore to God. Resist the devil and he will flee from you." (James 4:7, NASB)

Even in the dark times, God will give blessings. "I will give you the treasures of darkness and hidden wealth of secret places, so that you may know that it is I, The Lord, the God of Israel, who calls you by your name." (Isaiah 45:3, NASB)

God's peace flows forever. "For thus says the Lord, 'Behold, I extend peace to her like a river... Peace I leave with you; My peace I give to you; not as the world gives do I give to you. Do not let your heart be troubled, nor let it be fearful." (Isaiah 66:12, NASB), John 14:27, NASB)

God fights for us when the enemy comes against us. "... when the enemy comes in like a flood, The Spirit of the Lord will lift up a standard against him." (Isaiah 59:19, NKJV)

God is our rescuer. "He sent from above, He took me, He drew me out of many waters." (2 Samuel 22:17, NKJV)

"The Lord said: I will certainly set you free and care for you. I will certainly intercede for you in a time of trouble, in your time of distress, with the enemy." (Jeremiah 15:11, HCSB)

"For with God nothing is ever impossible and no word from God shall be without power or impossible of fulfillment." (Luke 1:37, AMPC)

"... Do not fear, for I have redeemed you; I have called you by name; you are Mine! When you pass through the waters, I will be with you; and through the rivers, they will not overflow you. When you walk through the fire, you will not be scorched, nor will the flame burn you. For I am the Lord your God, The Holy One of Israel, your Savior..." (Isaiah 43:1-3, NASB)

"Be strong and courageous, do not be afraid or tremble at them, for the Lord your God is the one who goes with you. He will not fail you or forsake you." (Deuteronomy 31:6, NASB)

Further verses and prayers are found at the end of the book. Remember always, God and His Word will set us free!

Busy, so very busy

Full-throttle, I hurry about the house. I need to do something – work on Bible-study, write, read, spend time with God, clean the house, do laundry, work in the yard, read, write, spend time with God.... I must do something. I need to fill every minute of time with something useful, don't I?

Must be busy and stay busy, so very busy. When I'm not moving, I feel guilty. I want to be a good servant for the Lord. So, doesn't that mean staying busy?

The words of Psalm 23 beckon, "*The Lord is my shepherd. I shall not want. He makes me lie down in green pastures. He leads me beside still waters. He restores my soul....*"

I hesitate. Stop for a moment, but then feel guilty stopping. On the Sabbath, I'll rest. God commanded resting on the Sabbath. I can do that. No guilt there. But, during the week? I must stay active or feel like I'm wasting God's time.

Again, scripture beckons... *He makes me lie down...*

I sit. But, then I start working while I sit. Argh! I realize this is a trust issue. Can I trust the Lord enough to not be busy?

The Lord is my shepherd. I shall not want. He makes me lie down in green pastures. He leads me beside still waters. He restores my soul....

I ponder... Green pastures are for rest and feeding. Still waters refresh and quench thirst. Both bring restoration. Busyness for the sake of staying busy causes tiredness and burnout.

I realize, I'm busy with self-effort instead of relying on God's leading and power. *"Not by might nor by power, but by My Spirit, says the Lord of hosts"* (Zechariah 4:6). Goodness, I need to stop trying everything in my own might and power. I am not mighty or powerful.

The Lord is my shepherd. I need to let The Shepherd lead, to lie down when He makes me lie down, to follow when (and where) He leads, and then I will receive restoration.

God wants our hearts more than He wants our activity. I need to replace busyness with nearness to God. It's God I want to please, and God I want to love above all else, and God is the one who restores my soul.

Before this could be published, my sweet hubby shared truth from Henry and Richard Blackaby's devotional, Experiencing God Day by Day.

"There are those who feel that they must be constantly laboring for the Lord in order to meet God's high standards. ... In our zeal to produce 'results' for our Lord, we sometimes become so intent on fruit production that we neglect abiding in Christ. We may feel that 'abiding' is not as productive or that it takes too much time away from our fruit production. Yet Jesus said that it is not our activity that produces fruit, it is our relationship with Him." ~ Henry and Richard Blackaby

I'm so sad. My busyness has kept me from the best.

Time spent resting and abiding with the Lord is never wasted. The invitation to rest and abide grows relationship, restoration, and fruit production. "I am the vine, you are the branches. He who abides in Me, and I in him, bears much fruit; for without Me you can do nothing." (John 15:5, NKJV)

Thank You, Father that You are my Shepherd. Forgive me for staying so busy. Forgive me for thinking my production is based on my own activity and my work. I can make lots of stuff, but my stuff is only hay and stubble and will be blown away by the winds of time. Lasting, sweet fruit comes from You. Help me to rest and drink deep of Your living waters as I abide in You.

The Lord is my shepherd. I shall not want. He makes me lie down in green pastures. He leads me beside still waters. He restores my soul. Happy sigh....

The Shepherd is beckoning. Will you abide and rest?

Henry and Richard Blackaby, *Experiencing God Day by Day*, B & H Publishing Group, Nashville, TN, p 120

Don't walk away

I posted something on a social site and had what I thought was a friendly conversation with a fellow believer. The person mentioned she'd taught Sunday school for years, been a leader in Bible study, and even written a Christian book.

However, as the discussion continued, the person turned nasty. My posting about heaven was agreeable, but the alternative for those who refuse the free gift of grace from Christ, was not. She took me to task for having the audacity of mentioning hell. She had chosen atheism because when God did not honor her Christian book with book sales, she turned away from Him.

I was shocked, and before I could formulate a response, she unfollowed me and disappeared into cyber-space. Oh, I could have shared the stories of so many who have labored, and continue to labor, for the Lord without seeing a return on their spiritual investment this side of heaven.

Disappointment, heartache, tragedy, suffering, trauma, and unexpected life-changes take a toll on many. Life is hard, and it is difficult to keep a firm faith when everything seems to be imploding. It's tough to move forward when prayers don't seem to be answered.

Jesus told the story of the farmer sowing seeds. The seed falling on rocky ground, "is like the person who hears the teaching and quickly accepts it with joy. But he does not let the teaching go deep into his life, so he keeps it only a short time. When trouble or persecution comes because of the teaching he accepted, he quickly gives up." Matthew 13:20-21, NCV)*

Following Jesus is not an easy journey. Paul warned, "In fact, everyone who wants to live a godly life in Christ Jesus will be persecuted." (2 Timothy 3:12, NIV)

Many claim to be Christian until something negative happens. There are those who walk away from God when trouble comes to them or the ones they love. Satan is constantly on the move, crouching, roaring like a lion to distract, dissuade, disgust, and disappoint as many as possible so that they will walk away, give up, and turn their backs on God.

What if Paul had walked away? Although he faithfully served God throughout his ministry, numerous times he was whipped, beaten, and stoned. He spent years in prisons, was ship-wrecked several times, and in danger most of his faith-walk. What if he had turned away from God?

It's easy to claim Christianity when life is good and everything is going great. To be honest, I would prefer an easy life. I don't know anyone who loves trials and persecution. However, without the difficulties, how would we know our faith was real and firm? If every time something bad happened, we turned our backs and walked away, I guess we'd be constantly turning and backing. Goodness, I would have been flipping and flopping most of my life. Fortunately, God never turns His back on us. His loving hands remain faithful.

When trials come and you're tempted to walk away, remember Satan is the one who wants you to turn from God. **Don't listen to the enemy.**

Trials are not punishment.

Amy Carmichael wrote, *"Trials are not 'chastisement'. No earthly father goes on chastising a loving child. That is a common thought about suffering, but I am quite sure it is a wrong thought. Paul's suffering were not that, nor are yours. They are battle wounds. They are signs of high confidence—honours. The Father holds His children very close to His heart when they are going through such rough places as this."*[iv]

Peter reminds us, "...trials will show that your faith is genuine. It is being tested as fire tests and purifies gold—though your faith is far more precious than mere gold. So when your faith remains strong through many trials, it will bring you much praise and glory and honor on the day when Jesus Christ is revealed to the whole world." (1 Peter 1:7, NLT)

If you are angry, hurt, disappointed, heartbroken, suffering, disillusioned, mad and hurt, whatever you are feeling, run to God. Take everything to Him, scream, cry and question. He will never be surprised or upset by your questions and emotions. Jesus said to come to Him like little children. Most children do not have a filter, they will ask any question, and they don't hide their feelings. Turn to God, freely talk with Him. Remember, He's the one who sent His Son so you would be eternally free, and He wants you to walk in freedom.

Instead of walking away, run to your Savior. His loving arms are always, always open wide.

"Come to Me, all you who labor and are heavy-laden and overburdened, and I will cause you to rest. [I will ease and relieve and refresh your souls.]" (Matthew 11:28, AMPC)

"My brothers and sisters, when you have many kinds of troubles, you should be full of joy, because you know that these troubles test your faith, and this will give you patience. Let your patience show itself perfectly in what you do. Then you will be perfect and complete and will have everything you need." (James 1:2-4, NCV)

Mind wash

The memory pounced, blindsided, and left me reeling. I stood trying to regain my thoughts.

Painful memories can't be changed, I can't alter what happened, and at times they leave me heart-broken and heart-sick. Oh, I need a mind wash. I need to forget that terrible thing that happened, that moment when my loved one took their final breath, the final cry I heard, the hurtful words that were said, the phone call that rocked my world. Oh, I need a mind wash!

Satan wants us to think we can't fix the thoughts, that they will always torment, and we'll never be able to firmly stand, heal, and move forward. The devil wants our focus to stay on the negatives that happened, the sins we committed, the terrible thing we've seen, done, or experienced.

How do we get those thoughts under control, stand firm, heal, and move forward? Run to The Truth. **Nothing is impossible for God**, nothing is too hard for Him, and His love is pure, holy, and unfailing. God's perfect love drives out fear – all fear – fear of that bad memory, fear of those bad thoughts.

The enemy wants the focus to stay on the bad things instead of focusing on God who makes **all things** new, who causes **all things** to work together for good. Satan is the destroyer, but **Jesus is the restorer**.

Jesus came to release captives, bring sight to the blind, and set free those who are oppressed.

We don't have to stay bound by the enemy, we don't have to be blinded by Satan's lies that we can never be free or healed, Jesus sets us free from oppressive thoughts, and free from the memories that seek to destroy us. Through the power of Christ that lives within us, we take thoughts and memories captive.

We have been given the mind of Christ, a mind well-balanced and controlled by the Spirit, and the mind set on the Spirit is life. The Holy Spirit breathes Christ's life within us, the mind of Christ within us, giving us the ability to reason, to stand firm and heal by the power of Christ.

When thoughts or memories come to mind, remember your mind is not defenseless. Christ who lives within you has all power and authority; you are never unprotected. Ask Him who makes all things new, to give you a new thought to replace that one, ask the Lord to replace the thought with His truth, His healing, and His restoration.

Heavenly Father, thank You for Your unfailing love. Thank You that nothing is impossible for You. Oh, Father the enemy is trying to distract me with thoughts that bring heartache and pain. Father, You care for Your children and Your love is perfect, so please in Your tender mercies and Your pure love, replace those thoughts with Your truth and Your healing.

Behind the darkest storm, the Son always shines, and Father, Your Son lives within me. Thank You that He sets me free and in Your perfect love I have nothing to fear. Help me to replace bad thoughts with thoughts of You and Your love. Thank You that there is no condemnation for those who are in Christ Jesus. Thank You that evil will be punished, and no weapon forged against me will prosper.

Grant me the ability to think beyond the past to remember the amazing present and future I have with You. Thank You that my loved ones who passed away, their last breath here on earth was the first breath into eternal life. Help me to think on that which is true, honorable, right, pure, lovely, things of good repute, excellence and worthy of praise.

Please give me a visual of You standing in the way of that memory and any thought the devil brings to mind. Heavenly Father, in the pureness of You and Your love You wash me clean, You remove the stains of the enemy's fingerprints, You remove the stain of sin, You set me free! Praise You, Lord!

"For God did not give us a spirit of timidity or cowardice or fear, but [He has given us a spirit] of power and of love and of sound judgment and personal discipline [abilities that result in a calm, well-balanced mind and self-control]." (2 Timothy 1:7, AMP)

"There is no fear in love, but perfect love drives out fear..." (1 John 4:18, NET)

"... the mind set on the Spirit is life and peace." (Romans 8:6, NASB)

"... we have the mind of Christ." (1 Corinthians 2:16, NET)

"for the weapons of our warfare are not human weapons but are made powerful by God for tearing down strongholds. We tear down arguments and every arrogant obstacle that is raised up against the knowledge of God, and we take every thought captive to make it obey Christ. ...." (2 Corinthians 10:4-6, NET Bible)

"...by the renewing of your mind [focusing on godly values and ethical attitudes], so that you may prove [for yourselves] what the will of God is, that which is good and acceptable and perfect [in His plan and purpose for you]." (Romans 12:2, AMP)

"Be anxious for nothing, but in everything by prayer and supplication with thanksgiving let your requests be made known to God. And the peace of God, which surpasses all comprehension, will guard your hearts and your minds in Christ Jesus. Finally, brethren, whatever is true, whatever is honorable, whatever is right, whatever is pure, whatever is lovely, whatever is of good repute, if there is any excellence and if anything worthy of praise, dwell on these things." (Philippians 4:6-8, NASB)

Mind games

My mind whirled with possible scenarios. If "this" thing happened, how would I respond? What would I need to do and say? If "that" thing happened, how would I respond, what would I need to do and say? The more I analyzed and worried, the less prepared I felt for what might happen.

Satan tries to get us to imagine possible scenarios, because the more we put ourselves in an imaginary situation, the more worked-up we will be if that situation happens. If we think someone will be hostile, and we go in with a hostile attitude we may cause the other person to react in a hostile manner. The devil twists and manipulates to get us to think negatively about anything and everyone.

The enemy's darts comes in various methods, and he knows how to attack our thoughts. He wants us exhausted physically, mentally, and spiritually. Mind games with the enemy are not games. The enemy is out to capture our thoughts so he can keep us captive in our thoughts.

God is the only one who knows the future, because He already is in the future. God's freedom is for every moment of every day. Be prepared for what is next by staying in God's word, for His truth sets you free.

The sword of the Spirit slashes through enemy lies. You don't have to play mind games with the enemy. Take every thought captive, check them by shining God's light and throw out any not in line with His truth.

Keep your mind focused on God and ask Him to prepare you for what may happen. Trust God, and turn your concerns into thoughts of praises by remembering....

If "this" happens, the Lord is there.

If "that" happens, the Lord is there.

No matter what happens, the Lord is there.

Heavenly Father, thank You that no matter what happens, You are there. You never leave or forsake Your children; You are here now, and You are there now. You are omnipresent, present always, all-powerful, all-mighty, just, and righteous. You never have to run to catch up, never surprised by what happens or what the enemy does.

Father, I praise You that if "that" thing happens, You are there, and if "this" thing happens, You are there. You already have in place what is needed for whatever comes next. Thank You, that in Your power I can take all thoughts captive and throw out any that do not honor You. Show me Your truth, Lord. Help me to look at everything, remembering You are always with me and will always be with me.

Thank You that You have the answer and solution for any conversation or situation that may come in the future. Praise You, Father! "You will keep in perfect peace all who trust in you, all whose thoughts are fixed on you!" I'm trusting You and fixing my thoughts on You. Thank You, Father!

(2 Corinthians 10:4-5, Isaiah 26:3, NLT)

Breathless expectation

I'll admit to whining as we waited for our house to sell. We were sad about leaving our church and our church friends, but we knew the Lord prompted the move, so we got ready to move.

At any moment, a call might come about a house showing, so we would rise early to keep the house clean and prepared. I love having a spiffy, clean house and I hoped and prayed the next owner would love our home. However, during the wait, I was patient one minute and the next impatient. I trust the Lord, but my wavering attitude showed work is needed in several areas.

Goodness, it would be so nice to see the heavenly calendar with time and dates so I could make plans. I would have known exactly when we'd get a contract on the house and when we could close and move.

However, I wondered would I truly relax in that knowledge? There is always more I want to know. The only way to rest, is in trusting the Lord with every step of the past, present, and future -- walking by faith and not by sight.

The faith walk is remembering God is faithful, He has our best interests at heart and His timing is always perfect.

Oswald Chambers shared, *"Certainty is the mark of the commonsense life—gracious uncertainty is the mark of the spiritual life. To be certain of God means that we are uncertain in all our ways, not knowing what tomorrow may bring. This is generally expressed with a sigh of sadness, but it should be an expression of breathless expectation. We are uncertain of the next step, but we are certain of God."* (Oswald Chambers, *My Utmost for His Highest*)

I have no idea what tomorrow will hold, everything in life is uncertain, but I have the best certainty and that is God. Because of the faithfulness and unfailing love of God, I should be living in state of breathless expectation.

The proper perspective, the joyous key to waiting in the uncertainty of life, is the reality that nothing is uncertain in the hands of God. He knows it all, He loves me best, and His plans will be the best. Yes! I'm giddy with joy and breathless in expectation.

"'For I know the plans I have for you,' declares the Lord, 'plans to prosper you and not to harm you, plans to give you hope and a future.'" (Jeremiah 29:11, NIV)

"I'm thanking you, God, from a full heart, I'm writing the book on your wonders. I'm whistling, laughing, and jumping for joy; I'm singing your song, High God." (Psalm 9:1-2, MSG)

What am I missing?

We continued to wait for our house to sell. Waiting is hard. I thought our move would come swiftly. I thought the Lord would have us list, move, and we would be settled in a brief time.

The longing for home, the longing to be settled continues. This would be my thirty-sixth move and, for however long the Lord allows, I'm ready to stop moving

The Lord prompted this move; therefore, I'm unsettled here. We are ready, the house is ready. I feel trapped in the wait although I'm free in Christ. My home is not here on earth, and I know the feeling of being truly and fully settled will never come until I am home with the Lord. I want to go home (here and in heaven). My heart is with God and my heart belongs with God.

Yet, I wonder, what am I missing by not living in the moment? The thing I'm wanting, hoping for, *will* come. My misery and whining won't help anything or anyone. I only miss today. I miss seeing God work in the here and now. I can't experience the now if I'm living in the past or in the future. The now is only experienced in the now.

Unsettled feelings come from looking at all that is unsettled. The settling of my soul comes from keeping my gaze focused on God. Only He is unchanging, unmoving, and unfailing. God is The Rock, the place where I am home. In His presence is fullness of joy. I don't want miss God. I don't want to miss His joy.

I don't want to miss today, for what I'm wanting, needing, longing for, is not a place, it's in the presence of God.

Don't miss today, don't miss the now. Rest in the home in God's loving heart.

"...we know that when these bodies of ours are taken down like tents and folded away, they will be replaced by resurrection bodies in heaven—God-made, not handmade—and we'll never have to relocate our 'tents' again. Sometimes we can hardly wait to move—and so we cry out in frustration. Compared to what's coming, living conditions around here seem like a stopover in an unfurnished shack, and we're tired of it! We've been given a glimpse of the real thing, our true home, our resurrection bodies! The Spirit of God whets our appetite by giving us a taste of what's ahead. He puts a little of heaven in our hearts so that we'll never settle for less.... When the time comes, we'll be plenty ready to exchange exile for homecoming. But neither exile nor homecoming is the main thing. Cheerfully pleasing God is the main thing, and that's what we aim to do, regardless of our conditions... " (2 Corinthians 5:1-10, MSG)

"You make known to me the path of life; you will fill me with joy in your presence, with eternal pleasures at your right hand." (Psalm 16:11, NIV)

Ready to roam

With contract in hand on our Tennessee home, a pre-approval letter from the bank, and a list of houses we wanted to see, sweet hubby and I drove to where we believed the Lord was leading us for our next move. The peak season for moving had hit and our Realtor in Alabama only had Friday to spend with us looking for houses.

Sweet hubby and I spent Thursday checking neighborhoods, driving by the homes we had on our list, and making note of the ones we wanted to see. By the time we met with the Realtor, we had narrowed the list from about twenty homes to three.

Meeting early in the morning, our agent drove us to our top choice. On the online realtor site, the pictures of the home had looked perfect. However, when we arrived, the house was much smaller, wasn't as well-maintained as it looked online, and the information was incorrect. Disappointed, we moved on to the next house on our list.

When we reached our second choice, we all walked around stunned at the many negative issues inside and out. We crossed that one off our list and drove to the next. House number three was perfect -- wonderfully maintained, well-loved, a beautiful small yard, and the right floor plan for now and as we get older. We were ecstatic and hurried back to the Realtor's office to put in a contract.

We placed an offer for a little less than they were asking, waited, then received a counteroffer with them wanting full price.

We felt this house was "the one" and the price was good, so we happily agreed. Based on our move date set here, we told them we would like the house in six weeks.

However, they replied they didn't know where they were going, and really weren't ready to move, so could we wait about two more months. What? I thought when someone put a house for sale they would actually want to sell and let the buyers take possession. Oh my. Obviously, there were decisions to be made. We had thirty days to get out of our house and the "sellers" wanted us to pay full price and wait until they are ready to move.

We wondered what would happen if we waited on the sellers? What would be the cost to store the furniture and stay in a hotel (or beg to stay with family members)? We couldn't get back to house-hunt until the next week which meant our time-window on finding a house was growing shorter by the day. What if we couldn't find another house in time?

Even with all the "what if" questions and uncertainty, we knew if God wanted us to have that house, things would work out and we would have that house. If God didn't want us to have that house, He had something better planned.

God isn't surprised by what happens, He always is in control, and His love never fails.

We had no idea what would happen next, but the situation reminded me of the times I've told God I would go wherever and whenever He wanted.

However, when the prompting came to move forward, I whimpered and hesitated. How many times have I said I would do something for the Lord but only because I was trying to be a "good" girl by making the offer? Oh dear. Not good. I need to make sure I am willing to obey God, and not just be willing to obey but actually obey.

As for our house issue, it was a crazy ride. We continued to pray, and do what we could, prepare however we could, look where we could, and be open to whatever God had planned.

We trusted God to guide and lead our steps. The Buffaloes knew we had to roam, we were willing to roam, we just weren't sure where were roaming. So, stay tuned for the next adventure of... *As The Buffaloes Roam.*

"A man's mind plans his way [as he journeys through life], but the Lord directs his steps and establishes them." (Proverbs 16:9, AMP)

"Many plans are in a man's mind, but it is the Lord's purpose for him that will stand (be carried out)." (Proverbs 19:21, AMP)

"Trust in and rely confidently on the Lord with all your heart and do not rely on your own insight or understanding. In all your ways know and acknowledge and recognize Him, and He will make your paths straight and smooth [removing obstacles that block your way]." (Proverbs 3:5-6, AMP)

Tender boundaries

Many times, I've felt caged by circumstances. Like a racehorse trapped at the starting gate, I have, cried, kicked and bashed against the confining boundaries. If only I could run free, I would be happy and satisfied.

My visual is not a pretty picture. Being antsy and frustrated at not being able to do what I want to do, or go where I want to go, have left my little racehorse-self battered and bruised.

Jesus says to come to Him and He will give us rest. I picture the Lord sitting and watching from the stands at the racetrack. I'm having a fit at not being able to run, but then I realize God placed the boundaries around me.

When I was younger and horrible things happened and no one was there to help, my Father God held me close and loved me back to life.

During times of illness and surgeries, when I couldn't do anything, I couldn't move physically, my spirit soared in the freedom of His presence. When I felt confined in a new location without friends and family, I discovered more of the friendship and relationship with God.

God's boundaries have kept me from making bad mistakes and from pursuing things I thought I wanted. His boundaries have kept me from things I thought I was ready to handle, but looking back I see how disastrous they would have been.

I still see myself as a little racehorse enclosed at the starting gate, but now the visual is an enclosure padded with His love. I'm standing, waiting, held tenderly tight in the freedom and unfailing love of God.

Feeling confined? Remember, God's boundaries are always tender with His love.

"Come to Me, all who are weary and heavy-laden, and I will give you rest. Take My yoke upon you and learn from Me, for I am gentle and humble in heart, and you will find rest for your souls. For My yoke is easy and My burden is light." (Matthew 11:28-30, NASB)

"The boundary lines have fallen for me in pleasant places; surely I have a delightful inheritance." (Psalm 16:6, NIV)

"You have enclosed me behind and before and laid Your hand upon me. Such knowledge is too wonderful for me; it is too high, I cannot attain to it." (Psalm 139:5-6, NASB)

Keep working

The hard work you do, the sacrifices you make, the constant giving of yourself and your skills, don't seem noticed. The accolades don't come, you've been passed over for the promotion, the family doesn't seem to care, and no one appears to understand how hard you work. Even God seems distant.

Working. Is. Hard. Shouldn't they, and shouldn't He, reward you? Shouldn't you at least get a "thank you" or a pat on the back? It's hard to keep working when no one seems to notice. It's hard when the reward we thought we would receive never comes to fruition.

When questions and doubts attack me, I wonder am I working for the praise of man or for God? Pleasing people is a trap, a snare. Working for the praise of man is an empty void that can never be filled, like trying to fill a cup with holes in the bottom.

If I work to satisfy my fleshly desires, to please others, to attain earthly treasure or earthly praise, all I've accomplished is temporary. Only Kingdom treasures are eternal treasures.

When I feel like giving up, I need to get my mindset back on God, on His purposes and His Kingdom. When I work for Him, keep my eyes on Him, then work is pleasure. Then, work becomes a blessing as I work to bless The One who has eternally blessed me.

To keep my thoughts on the right track, to get back on my feet, and my hands steady to stay at the work I believe the Lord has called me to complete, I run to God's Word. The Bible gives truth to replenish the weary soul and courage to continue.

Even when no one notices, remember God sees what is done in secret and will reward you. When it's hard, keep working, don't grow weary in doing good and remember even those who sow in tears will reap with joyful shouting.

Even when you are under attack from the enemy, remember the Lord is faithful, and He will strengthen and protect you from the evil one.

Stop paying attention to people and working to please others, don't fear them, listen to God, He will provide comfort, protection, and be faithful to help you complete the work He has given you. Don't work for selfish reasons and empty conceit, look for God's interests and the interests of others. Walk in a manner worthy of your calling, keep your hand on the plow and run the race to win the prize.

Remember, you are God's workmanship created in Christ Jesus for good works which God prepared beforehand. You are seated in the heavenly places, therefore, work for the kingdom of God. Work for God's glory shining your light for His glory, to please Him. Work with God, work for the Eternal for eternal purposes and eternal reward.

Be diligent to present yourself approved to God as a workman who doesn't need to be ashamed, accurately handling the word of truth.

God gives us victory through Jesus Christ. Don't be moved. Always be outstanding in your work for God.

Remember always, your labor for the Lord is never in vain. Keep working, friends. Keep working!

"Companions as we are in this work with you, we beg you, please don't squander one bit of this marvelous life God has given us. God reminds us, 'I heard your call in the nick of time; the day you needed me, I was there to help.' Well, now is the right time to listen, the day to be helped. Don't put it off; don't frustrate God's work by showing up late, throwing a question mark over everything we're doing. Our work as God's servants gets validated—or not—in the details. People are watching us as we stay at our post, alertly, unswervingly . . . in hard times, tough times, bad times; when we're beaten up, jailed, and mobbed; working hard, working late, working without eating; with pure heart, clear head, steady hand; in gentleness, holiness, and honest love; when we're telling the truth, and when God's showing his power; when we're doing our best setting things right; when we're praised, and when we're blamed; slandered, and honored; true to our word, though distrusted; ignored by the world, but recognized by God; terrifically alive, though rumored to be dead; beaten within an inch of our lives, but refusing to die; immersed in tears, yet always filled with deep joy; living on handouts, yet enriching many; having nothing, having it all. ... I can't tell you how much I long for you to enter this wide-open, spacious life. We didn't fence you in.

The smallness you feel comes from within you. Your lives aren't small, but you're living them in a small way. I'm speaking as plainly as I can and with great affection. Open up your lives. Live openly and expansively!" (2 Corinthians 6:5-13, MSG)

(Matthew 6:4, Psalm 126:5, Galatians 6:9, 2 Thessalonians 3:3, Isaiah 2:22, John 12:43, Isaiah 51:7, Isaiah 51:12, 1 Thessalonians 5:23-24, Philippians 1:6, Philippians 2:3-4, Ephesians 4:1, Luke 9:62, 1 Corinthians 9:24, Ephesians 2:10, Ephesians 2:5-7, Matthew 5:16, 2 Corinthians 5:5-6, 2 Corinthians 6:6, 1 Corinthians 3:13-14, 2 Timothy 2:15, 1 Corinthians 15:57-58)

Forever Family

Special days are set aside to celebrate fathers and mothers, which are times of joy for many and for others they are difficult.

For those who have lost fathers, had terrible fathers, or never knew their fathers, Father's Day is difficult. Whether your father was a blessing or not, please know, please always remember, you have a loving, tender, compassionate, merciful, Heavenly Father. Your Heavenly Father will never leave you or forsake you.

"He is a father to the fatherless and an advocate for widows. As a father has compassion on his children, so the Lord has compassion on his faithful followers" (Psalm 68:5, Psalm 103:13).

For those who have lost mothers, had terrible mothers, or for those who never knew their mothers, Mother's Day is difficult. Whether your mother was a blessing or not, please know, please always remember, you have a loving, tender, compassionate, merciful Heavenly Father who loves with the tender caring love of the best mother. Your heavenly Father's gentle love will never leave or forsake you.

"Can a woman forget her baby who nurses at her breast? Can she withhold compassion from the child she has borne? Even if mothers were to forget, I could never forget you!" As a mother consoles a child, so I will console you, and you will be consoled ..." (Isaiah 49:15-16, Isaiah 66:13).

For those who are orphans or who have been abandoned by those who should have given them a home, please know, always remember you are a child of a loving God safe at home in His heart.

"Even if my father and mother abandoned me, the Lord would take me in. The Spirit himself bears witness to our spirit that we are God's children See what sort of love the Father has given to us: that we should be called God's children—and indeed we are! (Psalm 27:10, Romans 8:16, 1 John 3:1)

God Himself, hands on, tender touch, created you unique and special because He loves you. He formed your inward parts and knitted you together in your mother's womb. God feels the pain you feel, the heartbreak that breaks your heart, the agony of love lost and lives lost, the pain that shreds the soul. God's comfort is boundless and complete, for His compassion never fails and is never every morning. The LORD is good, and his unfailing love lasts forever.

You were born by the love of God. God knit you together in your mother's womb, He knows your thoughts and thinks about you more than the grains of sand at the seashore. God sings over you while you sleep, hems you in behind and before, watches over you night and day, His goodness and mercy follow you and His mercies are new every morning. All days are ordained by God and His love is with you, for you, and will never fail you or forsake you. God loved you enough to die for you so you could live forever in His love. (Psalm 139:1-18, Psalm 23:6,

Zephaniah 3:17, Lamentations 3:22-23, Deuteronomy 31:8, John 3:16-17)

God will never abandon you, never leave you, never forsake you, for you are forever in His family and forever loved.

"Father of orphans, champion of widows, is God in his holy house. God makes homes for the homeless, leads prisoners to freedom... How blessed is God! And what a blessing he is! He's the Father of our Master, Jesus Christ, and takes us to the high places of blessing in him. Long before he laid down earth's foundations, he had us in mind, had settled on us as the focus of his love, to be made whole and holy by his love. **Long, long ago he decided to adopt us into his family through Jesus Christ. (What pleasure he took in planning this!)** He wanted us to enter into the celebration of his lavish gift-giving by the hand of his beloved Son." (Psalm 68:5-6, Ephesians 1:3-6, MSG) Emphasis added on scripture.

I Am with you

I'll be honest, I've been struggling. As my eyesight continues to worsen, my flesh is weak as my faith tries to stand strong. God tells us not to fear, and I try to be brave, I so try to be brave, but I am afraid. I know God will help; I know He will equip me to handle whatever comes. Perhaps my eyesight will be cured, perhaps not.

God says, "Do not fear," and thankfully He doesn't stop there, He reassures, "for I am with you" (Isaiah 41:10, Isaiah 43:5). God is a loving Father, when He tells us not to fear or worry, it's because God is with us, He is for us, and He will help us.

Fear will come, there are frightening things in this world, but our God is with us in the world. God's love is unfailing, He won't leave or forsake us, He knows we are but dust, and He understands our frailties.

When my flesh wobbles with worry, God's comfort flows through, His strong arms catch and surround me, and He will guide through the light and through the dark. I don't need to concentrate on the fear of what may come, or what may happen, instead I need to remember God is with me. God is the deliverer, healer, restorer, and redeemer. What have I to fear when God is with me? Nothing. Absolutely nothing. Praise God, He is with me!

Friend, whatever you face, whatever may come in your future, remember **God is with you**.

As a good Father steadies His young child who is trying to walk, God hold us tight and steadies us through the hard times. If illness attacks you, enemies surround you, difficulties assail you, there is nothing too big, nothing impossible, nothing beyond the reach of our all-powerful, loving God.

Don't be afraid for <u>He is with you</u>, and He will be with you. Praise God, The Great I AM is with you!

"Do not fear, for I am with you; do not anxiously look about you, for I am your God. I will strengthen you, surely I will help you, surely I will uphold you with My righteous right hand. Do not be afraid of them, for I am with you to deliver you,' declares the Lord. When you pass through the waters, I will be with you; and through the rivers, they will not overflow you. When you walk through the fire, you will not be scorched, nor will the flame burn you. For I am the Lord your God, The Holy One of Israel, your Savior..." (Isaiah 41:10, Jeremiah 1:8, Isaiah 43:2-3, NASB)

Not going to stop the joy

I wrote earlier about being afraid with my worsening eyesight. The eyesight issues are a long troublesome list, it's getting harder to see fine print, the world is getting grayer by the day. And man, it's hard not to have moments of worry regarding those facts. However, I refuse to allow those issues to ruin my life. I refuse to stop God's joy from flowing.

The other night I went to a painting class with church friends. I'll be honest, after I had shared about my eyesight issues, I almost felt guilty posting a picture on Facebook of me having fun. What would people think if they saw me enjoying life? Would they think I overexaggerated my eye problems? Shouldn't I be sitting in a corner with a sad face? (Okay, I do that sometimes). I've been through some really rough stuff in my life and God is teaching me (and continues teaching me) how to live in victory.

The battle over fear is a constant struggle for most of us who live in this crazy world. The early church went through horrific persecution and yet the letters from the apostles told them again and again to be joyful. Joyful? What's up with that? How can someone have joy when run out of homes and business, fed to lions, burned at the stake, stoned, and a long list of terrible difficulties? Their request to the early church didn't make sense, it doesn't make sense, to tell someone to have joy through trials. And yet, Christianity **is** joy through trials -- joy through the good, bad, and terribly ugly.

We can have joy regardless of what has happened, what is happening, and what may happen because of Jesus. With Jesus in our hearts, our hearts are always safe, and His joy flows forever.

Joy isn't something we have to manufacture or muster up our strength and plaster on a fake smile, **joy constantly and consistently flows from God's throne**.

Nehemiah tells us the joy of the Lord is our strength. **God's joy** gives us strength. **God's joy** is there for us, and with us, through everything. **God's joy** brings comfort, healing, restoration, relationship, blessings, gifts, equipping, and eternal love.

The world expects us to act and react in certain ways. Yet, we aren't of this world. We aren't confined to this world and the world's ways. We are forever free in Christ, living in His eternal love and His mighty power. Regardless of what is going on with us, or around us, we have hope in Christ and the joy of the Lord.

God works ALL things for the good for those who love Him and are called according to His purpose. So, I'm believing and trusting that ALL things are going to work for good with my eyesight. He will either heal me or walk me through another hardship, and either way I'm on the winning team. I refuse to let the devil steal or stop my joy!

Let God's joy flow free!

"Rejoice in the Lord always; again I will say, rejoice!" for "we know that God causes all things to work together for good to those who love God, to

those who are called according to His purpose."
(Philippians 4:4, NASB), Romans 8:28, NASB)

The Door Home

My thirty-sixth move loomed on the horizon. Every move brought excitement, hesitation, negatives, and positives. Each new city offered opportunities for lessons and growth as life-long friendships and sweet family memories were made. As we moved again and again, I hoped and prayed I would finally find home – not just a house, but **home**.

I pondered this continual desire for home, and I realized Jesus is the way Home, He is the door. Jesus is the door Home!

No matter how many times I move, the Door Home stays open through Jesus Christ. *Happy sigh*

The amazing, wonderful thing is, there is so much more in God's word about the word "door."

Jesus is the door (John 10:7-9) Jesus stands at the door, and is the way to grace, mercy, and abundant life (Revelation 3:20).

God opens doors to set captives free, to open the door of salvation, to open doors of ministry, to open doors no man can shut (Luke 4:18, John 10:7-10, 1 Corinthians 16:9, Revelation 3:7).

Passover, where death passes over the door and Jesus is the Passover lamb to free us from eternal death (Exodus 12:7, Exodus 12:22-23, John 1:29).

We are told to keep and write God's word on the doorposts of our houses (Deuteronomy 6:9, 11:20). To close our doors and pray to the Father (Matthew 6:6).

The door is an ark (refuge, safety, rescue) (Genesis 7:15-16).

God met to speak at the door of the tabernacle (Exodus 29:42, Exodus 33:9-10). The Lord appeared at the tabernacle in a pillar of cloud, standing above the door (Deuteronomy 31:15). Moses and Aaron went to the door of the tabernacle, fell on their faces and the glory of the Lord appeared to them at the door. (Numbers 20:6).

Sin crouches at the door and its desire is for you, but you should rule over it (Genesis 4:7).

Jesus, The Door, opens our lives to an incredible, grace-filled, mercy of eternal life. Jesus is the door to release us from captivity of sin and worry. Jesus is the door for our ministry here on earth, doors that no man can shut. Jesus is the Passover lamb that takes away our sin, He is the door to our Heavenly Father.

Are you looking for the door home? Enter through The Door and you are always Home.

"I am the Door; anyone who enters through Me will be saved [and will live forever], and will go in and out [freely], and find pasture (spiritual security)." (John 10:9, AMPC)

Disadvantaged and disabled

Scientific studies show when vision is lost, hearing and the sense of touch are heightened. I wonder what God has gifted to compensate for other losses in our lives? What will be gained? Paul writes to the Ephesians praying for the eyes of their heart to be enlarged. Oh, yes! Even when earthly eyesight grows dim, soul-vision grows without measure.

God's Kingdom is greater, mightier, and more amazing than we can imagine. We walk by faith not by sight. Faith is what we hope for, what we cannot see, existing beyond our earthly senses. God's ways are not our ways and are always the best for us and for His kingdom.

Even a disadvantaged disability is not a problem for God. Nothing is impossible for Him, and He has equipped us to handle whatever each day holds. What the enemy means for evil, God turns to good for those who love Him. For the Christian, every negative comes with a positive.

God's glory is often hidden in difficulty. God uses the weak, those who can't accomplish what they are called to accomplish without His help, to display His glory.

God's glory is displayed as the small become mighty in God's power. His glory comes as the disadvantaged conquer the advantaged. God's glory comes as our lack of ability is turned into God-given ability. His glory comes as we are eternally compensated no matter what the loss here on earth.

Inside every disadvantage and disability is an opportunity to display the over-coming ability and amazing advantage of those who are in Jesus Christ.

Are you disabled? Disadvantaged? You, my friend, have been given every advantage and ability to display God's power, might, and His glory!

"Now faith is the assurance (title deed, confirmation) of things hoped for (divinely guaranteed), and the evidence of things not seen [the conviction of their reality—faith comprehends as fact what cannot be experienced by the physical senses] ... for we walk by faith, not by sight]." (Hebrews 11:1, AMP), 2 Corinthians 5:7, NASB)

"The Lord will accomplish what concerns me; Your lovingkindness, O Lord, is everlasting...." (Psalm 138:8, NASB)

I pray "that the God of our Lord Jesus Christ, the Father of glory, may give to you the spirit of wisdom and revelation in the knowledge of Him, the eyes of your understanding being enlightened; that you may know what is the hope of His calling, what are the riches of the glory of His inheritance in the saints, and what is the exceeding greatness of His power toward us who believe, according to the working of His mighty power." (Ephesians 1:17-19, NKJV)

Bluebird blessings

In the two years we lived in Tennessee, we were blessed to watch the nesting and hatching of two Bluebird families. The day before we moved, I sat at my office chair to have a quiet moment before I continued packing. Looking out the window I noticed the clouds moving at a rapid pace. Curious, I watched and wondered. Then, in my spirit, I felt a gentle nudge to go outside and spend time with God.

Settling in a patio chair, I gazed at the sky. Movement and chirping drew my attention. Mom and Dad Bluebird, who had just recently completed their last family, had come by for a visit. Since their family had left, they hadn't been around very much, and I missed their presence.

The birds chirped and spread their wings while they talked, and I wondered if they were trying to communicate with me. I smiled considering the goodness of God to bless me with seeing them again and experiencing such a sweet moment. If I hadn't noticed the clouds, if I had ignored the gentle prompting to go outside, I would have missed the Bluebird blessing.

How many times are God's blessings missed? Every day, each moment, God reveals Himself in wonderful ways, but we must take time to notice. Taking time, making time, opening our eyes and ears, our spirits to see, hear, and acknowledge God's blessings bless us with the ability to experience God's blessings.

Our Heavenly Father is a good, loving Father and His gifts of love continuously flow from His throne. Today, each day, you are given blessings by God. Don't miss the joy of God's blessings. The blessings might come in the chirping of a bird, the fragrance of a flower, or in a myriad of ways that bring a smile to your face and a lift to your spirit. Watch, notice, and be blessed!

"Every good thing given, and every perfect gift is from above, coming down from the Father of lights, with whom there is no variation or shifting shadow." (James 1:17, NASB)

"O praise the Lord, all you nations! Praise Him, all you people! For His mercy and loving-kindness are great toward us, and the truth and faithfulness of the Lord endure forever. Praise the Lord! (Hallelujah!)." (Psalm 117, AMPC)

Breaking bitterness

Bitterness, anger, unforgiveness, rehearsing, remembering, ruminating about the negative things in life only drives a stake of lead into one's soul, leeching, poisoning, bringing additional pain to you and others and colors everything in darkness.

Jesus says forgive others and **you** will be forgiven. Forgiving others doesn't let the ones who hurt you, who did you wrong, off the hook it frees you from the hooks of anger, bitterness, and resentment. Forgiveness of others cleanses you, releases you, unchains you, and allows the light of Christ to remove the dark stains left by dark memories.

Whatever you gripe about, grips you in its grasp. Holding on to the wrong things, holds you into the wrong things. When you are fixated on the past, you become fixed to the past. Instead of being angry about what was, be grateful for what is. Instead of complaining about yesterday be grateful for today.

Whatever ways the devil has messed with you through the actions of others or the negative things of life, don't give him another minute of satisfaction. Don't allow Satan to keep tormenting you. Break free of the bitterness and anger by releasing everything into the loving grasp of God. God is just and righteous, He will repay those who have done wrong. God's love makes all things new, restores, redeems, cleanses, makes the impossible possible, and **sets you free**.

"When angry, do not sin; do not ever let your wrath (your exasperation, your fury or indignation) last until the sun goes down. And do not give the devil an opportunity [to lead you into sin by holding a grudge, or nurturing anger, or harboring resentment, or cultivating bitterness]." (Ephesians 4:26, AMPC), Ephesians 4:27, AMP)

"For if you forgive people their trespasses [their reckless and willful sins, leaving them, letting them go, and giving up resentment], your heavenly Father will also forgive you. But if you do not forgive others their trespasses [their reckless and willful sins, leaving them, letting them go, and giving up resentment], neither will your Father forgive you your trespasses." (Matthew 6:14-15, AMPC)

It all turned out okay

Our house in Tennessee was originally scheduled to close on Monday, July 3rd in Tennessee, and Alabama. Movers were scheduled to pick us up June 30th and deliver our belongings on July 5th. Since we were leaving town before closing, we setup an early signing for the documents at the title company on June 29th. We also scheduled to have carpeting replaced in two bedrooms at the house we were buying early on the morning of July 5th. All went smooth with the early signing and the movers loaded our belongings. We closed out the house and drove to Alabama to stay with relatives.

Then, the buyers had a problem with paperwork and changed the official close date to a few days later. We contacted our movers, rescheduled them for delivery on the 6th and set up another close date in Alabama. The carpet guys moved their date to the morning of the 6th, and the internet provider had to change their date for another week.

The new close date was set, but when we went to close on the new place in Alabama, the lender wouldn't approve going further without proof the Tennessee house had sold. However, we couldn't find our Realtor (he had gone on vacation and was out of cell-phone range). And, the person at the title company in Tennessee couldn't find out when the close was actually going to happen. So, we had to shut down everything.

Fortunately, the sellers in Alabama were kind enough to rent us the house on a week-by-week schedule until we could close. The carpet guys installed the carpet, and the movers delivered the furniture.

Then, the buyers in Tennessee sent paperwork saying the close date now had been moved to July 11th. The Title company here in Alabama rescheduled the close on July 12th. And FINALLY, both houses closed, and funds were transferred. Yay!!!

During the turmoil, phone calls, date moving, rescheduling, wondering, waiting, and craziness, God took wonderful care of us. Sweet hubby's brother and wife were generous enough to let us stay with them. Everyone on the Alabama end worked with us during schedule and plan changes. The Tennessee Title company continually tried to find out information for us as the dates kept changing. Our Alabama Realtor was wonderful to help us through all the uncertainty. And, the seller here worked with us without any issues or problems. We were abundantly blessed by God's kindness.

The house, yard, and neighborhood are wonderful, and we've already found a church home and we are settling into the home God has given us. We are blessed, blessed, blessed!

God is in His kindness also had me wait to post about this adventure. To be honest, during the uncertainty, I wanted to scream, rant and rave about the constant delays and problems. I'm grateful we didn't have internet service during that time.

I wish I could tell you I kept calm and controlled during it all, but I didn't. During the bumps, some unsightly thoughts and actions came out of my bumped body.

If I had known how it would turn out, that all would be okay, that everything would work out, I would have been a calm, delightful person.

Regardless of what was happening, I should have remembered God would take care of us. He always has, He always will.

Fortunately, God is gracious. His kindness flowed through, His provision continued, His mercy remained unfailing.

Are you encountering unwelcome changes in your plans and bumps along your journey? God has you. He knows your needs. God understands the difficulties of life. He'll be with you. Forever, He will be with you, and it will turn out okay. He promises.

And in the end, we will all stand and marvel at how it all turned out okay.

"When you pass through the waters, I will be with you; and through the rivers, they will not overflow you. When you walk through the fire, you will not be scorched, nor will the flame burn you. For I am the Lord your God, The Holy One of Israel, your Savior... For I know the plans that I have for you, declares the Lord, 'plans for welfare and not for calamity to give you a future and a hope." (Jeremiah 29:11, NASB), Isaiah 43:2-3, NASB)

"And we know that God causes **all things to work together for good** to those who love God, to

those who are called according to His purpose."
(Romans 8:28, NASB)

Show me

The difficulties of life stink. When those we hoped were trustworthy take away our trust and losses leak holes in our hearts, if we aren't careful, if we don't take our burdens to Jesus, those hard things can leave hard places in our souls.

I know pain, I understand many of life's hard things, I've been molested by a baby-sitter, assaulted by two guys, raped, and stalked. I've been divorced, dealt with over eleven years of chronic illness, eight surgeries, and many, many other nasty and tough things. God has healed, restored, redeemed, and helped me through, and over, each difficulty. Our God is a good God, He takes what the enemy meant for evil and turns it into good for those who love Him.*

No matter what we go through, God helps us through. Jesus came to heal the brokenhearted and "announce release (pardon, forgiveness) to the captives, and recovery of sight to the blind, to set free those who are oppressed (downtrodden, bruised, crushed by tragedy)."*

However, when in the midst of trauma and heartache, when we have gone through things the world says we will never get over, remember God's word is truth. Jesus shows us how to heal, how to get through, how to get up one more day and take one more breath. Jesus sets captives free – completely and totally free. God's truth removes the blinders from our eyes, the hardness from our hearts, and sets us free in the light of His love.

Now when life hits hard and it's difficult to stand, pray and ask God ... from this situation, from every situation, Heavenly Father show me how to get through one more day.

Help me to see Your loving hand during this difficulty.

Grant me the ability to remember You are always with me.

Remind me of Your truth and show me Your truth in Your word.

Show me how to win against the enemy with Your power and Your truth.

Show me how to take captive these negative thoughts and negative memories.

Help me discover what You want me to know.

Show me Your goodness and loving-kindness.

Show me Your power.

Show me what I can learn.

Show me how I can grow.

Show me how I can develop as a Christian.

Show me ways I can help others through my own difficulties.

Show me, teach me, grow me, develop me, and make me more like Your precious Son, Jesus Christ.

Thank You, Father that You never leave or forsake us. Thank You that You are just and righteous and nothing is too hard or impossible for You. Show me, remind me, help me to always remember, no matter what happens, I am always forever safe in Your loving heart.

"Call to Me, and I will answer you, and show you great and mighty things, which you do not know." (Jeremiah 33:3, NKJV

"Show me Your ways, O Lord; teach me Your paths." (Psalm 25:4, NKJV)

"Show Your marvelous lovingkindness by Your right hand, O You who save those who trust in You from those who rise up against them." (Psalm 17:7, NKJV)

"Show me a sign for good, that those who hate me may see it and be ashamed, because You, Lord, have helped me and comforted me." (Psalm 86:17, NKJV)

"You will show me the path of life; in Your presence is fullness of joy; at Your right hand are pleasures forevermore." (Psalm 16:11, NKJV)

*Romans 8:28, Luke 4:18

Better than the dream

My dream has always been to own a cabin in the mountains, a log home with a river or stream where I could walk in the trees or sit by the water and commune with God. Throughout my life, I prayed, watched, waited, cried, begged, pleaded, and hoped that one day the dream would come to fruition.

Sweet hubby and I took road trips to destinations where we thought we would like to retire. We prayed, looked online, drove country roads, and searched, yet nothing gave us peace and confirmation from the Holy Spirit. We continued to wait and pray until finally, after the long journey, God opened the door for our retirement home.

The home He gave us is in a subdivision and looks like your typical brick Southern home built in the early 2000's with trees in the back yard. The property doesn't seem to meet the criteria I had prayed for, the dream I thought would come true. However, God granted the desires of my heart in a way far better and more appropriate for this stage of my life. With my weakening eyesight, living in the mountains on a large piece of property would be a problem.

The visual of what I thought I wanted, isn't what God granted -- He gave something much better. God blessed with a home sitting on a little hill in a very nice subdivision with a drainage easement in the back

I hope we can convert to look like a stream. We're turning the formal dining area with large picture windows into my office where I have plenty of light to read, study, and write.

The house and yard are perfect for us, and we feel as though we are on a permanent vacation. My heart is blessed and filled with the goodness and loving-kindness of our wonderful God.

Do you have a dream, a heart-desire? The Psalmist tells us to delight in the Lord and He will give us the desires of our heart. God's plans, His ways, are better than we can imagine. Trust Him. Delight in God, commit yourself to Him and watch the wonderful ways He will work.

"'For I know what I have planned for you,' says the Lord. 'I have plans to prosper you, not to harm you. I have plans to give you a future filled with hope.'" (Jeremiah 29:11, NET)

"'For My thoughts are not your thoughts, nor are your ways My ways,' says the Lord. 'For as the heavens are higher than the earth, so are My ways higher than your ways, and My thoughts than your thoughts.'" (Isaiah 55:8-9, NKJV)

"Trust in the Lord and do good; dwell in the land and cultivate faithfulness. Delight yourself in the Lord; and He will give you the desires of your heart. Commit your way to the Lord, trust also in Him, and He will do it." (Psalm 37:3-5, NASB)

Taking back the land

At one time, the yard with our home had been loved. Plantings of Crepe Myrtle, flowers, and decorative shrubbery are evidence of the care the lawn had once received. However, with the passing of time, undergrowth took over, trees grew wild, briers, poison ivy, and poison oak grew unabated, ticks moved in, snakes slithered, and the land became overgrown.

We stay busy trying to regain control of the property. After spraying ourselves thoroughly with anti-tick spray and covering our bodies with material to protect against the poison ivy and oak, we take our yard tools -- machete, ax, weed-eater, hedge clippers, bush-hog, and various others – and slowly take back the land. Much remains to be done, to keep things under control. Fortunately, we love what God has given us, we love being outside and working and seeing the fruits of our labor. The work is hard but very rewarding.

In the same way, the Israelites were told to drive out the enemies who lived in their promised land. They had to take action against evil, but the Israelites became complacent, ignored the enemy and didn't implicitly follow God's directions. What wasn't removed, became a thorn, snare, and continued heartache.

Our world is being overtaken by the enemy. Satan spreads weeds of discord, fear, anger, and evil.

We've got to take back the land.

If we don't love God, respond to live the way He commands, the enemy wins ground. To work to reclaim the land, we can't do it alone, but we can work together with God's power.

Let's humble ourselves, turn from sin, and remember our first love by loving the Lord our God with all our hearts, all our souls, and all our minds (Matthew 22:37).

Let's read God's Word to renew our minds, to get our focus back on God's kingdom and seek Him above all else. Let's pray and be active in helping others by ministering to the lost world and our Christian brothers and sisters.

Let's remain diligent to complete the work God has called us to complete, for His burden is easy and His yoke is light. Let's joyfully stay in love with the Lord, casting our cares on Him because He cares for us.

The land is messy and overrun, but nothing is impossible for our God, nothing is too hard for Him, and we can do all things through Christ who strengthens us. To the land, friends! To the land!

"If My people who are called by My name will humble themselves, and pray and seek My face, and turn from their wicked ways, then I will hear from heaven, and will forgive their sin and heal their land." (2 Chronicles 7:14, NKJV)

Insecurity

Sweet hubby and I watched an old movie with Audrey Hepburn. Stately, elegant, beautiful yet approachable, Audrey Hepburn. The next day, insecurity jumped all over me. I don't look like Audrey Hepburn, my hair isn't as cute as hers, and I can barely walk straight in high heels. Whimper.

Comparing myself to Audrey was not a smart move. I'll be honest, I wasted an entire day internally whining about my inadequacies. The more I thought about her and her beauty, the more I compared myself to her, the more insecure I became.

What was I thinking? Audrey Hepburn was an actress with perfect lighting, professional makeup artists, tailor-made clothing, and scripted dialogue. Under those conditions, I probably could look and act pretty good myself.

Insecurity is a tool from the enemy to keep us so self-focused we can't see reality and the beauty of our God created uniqueness. Insecurity keeps us from enjoying today, enjoying God, and enjoying others.

I want to get rid of insecurity by remembering I am **in** the eternal **security** of Jesus. It's not about being conformed to the image of an actress or person, but about conforming to the image of Christ.

The good news is, as a Christian, the process is an inward change, we are predestined to be conformed, called, justified, and glorified.

The change is inward, taking place within the soul radiating out, transforming, renewing, redeeming, making whole – wholly loved, wholly accepted, and wholly restored.

Insecure? Remember you are **secure in** Christ. You don't have to look to other people, compare yourself to others, but keep focused on Jesus, He is the author and perfecter, The One who takes and makes you His beautiful, transformed, renewed, glorified, wonderful work of art.

"For we are His workmanship [His own master work, a work of art], created in Christ Jesus [reborn from above—spiritually transformed, renewed, ready to be used] for good works, which God prepared [for us] beforehand [taking paths which He set], so that we would walk in them [living the good life which He prearranged and made ready for us]." (Ephesians 2:10, AMP)

"For those whom He foreknew, He also predestined to become conformed to the image of His Son, ... and these whom He predestined, He also called; and these whom He called, He also justified; and these whom He justified, He also glorified." Therefore, "fixing our eyes on Jesus, the author and perfecter of faith ... do not be conformed to this world, but be transformed by the renewing of your mind, so that you may prove what the will of God is, that which is good and acceptable and perfect." (Romans 8:29-30, NASB), Hebrews 12:2, NASB), Romans 12:2, NASB)

Rescue team

During World War II, the German army had conquered and pushed back the Allied forces. Over a period of nine days an incredible rescue of more than 330,000 troops took place off the beaches of Dunkirk. German Luftwaffe aircraft strafed and bombed the men, docks, and boats, while the RAF flew over 3,500 flights to protect troops.

Troops on the beaches, neck-deep in water, and on docks, were vulnerable to enemy fire. Desperate to get the men rescued, the call went out for private vessels to help with the evacuation. Around 700 ships took to the seas. Fishing boats, pleasure cruisers, ferries, and other small boats acted as shuttles to and from larger ships, and to safety on English shores.

What could have been total disaster, complete annihilation of the Allied forces, turned into a show of courage, bravery, and willingness to risk everything for the rescue of their fellow countrymen.

Like the boats that rescued the soldiers at Dunkirk, we need to be brave, bold, courageous, and help those trapped in enemy territory. Every day, every moment, the enemy is taking captives. Satan is killing, stealing, and destroying.

People are floundering neck-deep in sin, looking, wondering if there is anyone who will help and show them the way to freedom.

Jesus Christ came to rescue us, to set us free, let's remember to use our freedom to show others the way for their freedom. Be part of the rescue team storming the gates of hell and snatch the lost out of the fire.

We can rescue by land, sea, and air. Our feet travel to share the good news, our prayers wing through the air. The need is great, the call is immense, but our God is victorious, and we work in the power of **His** power.

As we rise in action, our fellow brothers and sisters in Christ are also encouraged to take action. Link hands, link faith shields, and get in the boat to be part of the rescue team!

"Preach the word [as an official messenger]; be ready when the time is right and even when it is not [keep your sense of urgency, whether the opportunity seems favorable or unfavorable, whether convenient or inconvenient, whether welcome or unwelcome]; correct [those who err in doctrine or behavior], warn [those who sin], exhort and encourage [those who are growing toward spiritual maturity], with inexhaustible patience and [faithful] teaching." (2 Timothy 4:2, AMP)

"Go therefore and make disciples of all the nations, baptizing them in the name of the Father and the Son and the Holy Spirit teaching them to observe all that I commanded you; and lo, I am with you always, even to the end of the age." (Matthew 28:19-20, NASB)

Gathered Home

While rereading Genesis the other day, this verse stood out ... "Abraham breathed his last and died in a ripe old age, an old man and satisfied with life; and he was gathered to his people." (Genesis 25:8, NASB) Abraham died and was gathered to his people. Isaac, Jacob, and others are mentioned at their deaths that they also were gathered to their people.

Death is not the end. Death leads to life. For those who follow God, death leads to the biggest and best homecoming of all. Our loved ones, those who have gone before us, were gathered tenderly, sweetly, and with exceeding joy as they came home.

For, precious in the sight of the Lord is the death of His godly ones. The righteous man perishes ...the righteous man is taken away from evil, he enters into peace (Psalm 116:15, Isaiah 57:1-2).

God's people wait to welcome home family. Those who love us, our people (God's people) wait at the pearly gates to gather us home. Happy sigh...

Jesus is the life, the truth, and the way home. As a Christian, "we are not afraid but are quite content to die, for then we will be at home with the Lord." (2 Corinthians 5:8, TLB)

We come home to our Savior and are gathered to our people. "and He will wipe away every tear from their eyes; and there will no longer be any death; there will no longer be any mourning, or crying, or pain; the first things have passed away." (Revelation 21:4, NASB)

The blessing of prayer

Many of you are battling and encountering difficulties along your journey. We are given the blessing of prayer, a lifeline to talk with the One who gave us life.

Whatever your concern, whatever you face, you can talk to God. God cares, He loves you, and He wants to hear from you. He made your voice, and He loves when you speak with Him.

"There are, and there ought to be, stated seasons of communion with God when, everything else shut out, we come into His presence to talk to Him and to let Him speak to us; and out of such seasons springs that beautiful habit of prayer that weaves a golden bond between heaven and earth." ~ E. M. Bounds

We have the gift of communication with our minds and our voice, a golden bond between heaven and earth where we can talk with God. "Call to Me, and I will answer you, and show you great and mighty things, which you do not know" (Jeremiah 33:3 NKJV). God wants to meet with you, just as He met with Adam and Eve in the garden of Eden, He wants to walk and talk with you.

Sometimes when my heart is hurting, I have a tough time knowing what to pray. Fortunately, the Holy Spirit intercedes for us, translating in love our requests to our Heavenly Father (Romans 8:26).

"Let us pray for the Spirit of prayer. He will take us into the workshop where the power conduits lie. Above the door of this room is writing, 'Nothing shall be impossible unto you.'" ~ O. Hallesby

Prayer lightens the weight of difficulties.

Prayer readjusts the focus from our problems to our mighty, unfailing God.

Prayer invites miracles.

Prayer brings hope.

Prayer prepares souls to receive God's message.

Prayer tenders us to hear God's whispers in the midst of life's business or problems, heartaches, and pain.

"God shapes the world by prayer. The more praying there is in the world, the better the world will be and the mightier the forces against evil everywhere. Prayer, in one phase of its operation, is a disinfectant and a preventive. It purifies the air; it destroys the contagion of evil." ~ E. M. Bounds[v]

Prayer ushers us into the presence of a God Who "by in consequence of the action of **His power** that is at work within us, is able to carry out **His purpose** and do **superabundantly, far over and above all that we dare ask or think infinitely beyond** our highest prayers, desires, thoughts, hopes, or dreams" (Ephesians 3:20 AMP). (bold mine)

Are you having a tough time finding the words to give voice to your prayers? God's word contains the power of His Word. When we pray with God's Word, God's power is released.

The Psalms often give voice to my concerns. David spoke his mind and didn't hesitate to come to God with how he was feeling and what he was thinking. He knew God's ears are attentive to the cries of God's children, and David knew how to cry out. We can do the same.

There is power when we pray -- really pray and intercede. Pray for the persecuted Christians. Pray for the lost. Pray for protection of those who love and follow Christ. Pray for a humble spirit before God to be bold in word, deed, and action for Christ

Prayers have merit in battles that rage in the spiritual realm. Pray for our leaders, that they would inquire of the Lord, seek God's wisdom and guidance. Pray for our leaders, that they would seek God's leadership.

Please pray. Pray for one another. Pray for those you love. Pray for those who you meet in your daily walk. Pray without ceasing.

Pray and keep the smoke rising! "Another angel came and stood at the altar, holding a golden pan for incense. He was given much incense to offer with the prayers of all God's holy people. The angel put this offering on the golden altar before the throne. The **smoke** from the incense went up from the angel's hand to God with **the prayers of God's people**." Revelation 8:3-4, NCV)

Are you having problems staying awake and alert when you pray? "Devote yourselves to prayer, **keeping alert** in it **with** an attitude of **thanksgiving**" (Colossians 4:2 NASB). Thanksgiving is the key! Pray with thanksgiving that God hears our prayers and we can approach the throne of grace with every need.

Keep praying, friends. You have been blessed with the power of prayer, the beauty of communicating with your Heavenly Father.

Please pray!

On the next few pages, I've comprised prayers and verses to hopefully provide comfort, peace, and help for the battles and concerns you face.

Prayer for today

Heavenly Father thank You for another day. We praise You and thank You for who You are. Your love reaches above the heavens. Your mercies are new every morning. Regardless of what we face, regardless of what has happened to us in the past, regardless of what will happen in the future, You are in control, and You are just, righteous, and merciful.

Heavenly Father, reveal the enemy lies that keep us in bondage. Reveal anything that keeps us from You.

Oh, Father, may we know You more, serve You more, love You more, obey and follow You completely. Help us to love You with the unfailing love with which You love.

Help us to live in Your Truth, to walk in Your Way, and to live freely in Your Life. Free us Lord, to be used freely for You!

Prayer for the lost

Heavenly Father, You are gracious, righteous, merciful, compassionate, slow to anger and great in lovingkindness. Peter wrote that You are patient not wanting anyone to perish, but everyone to come to repentance. Oh Father, my heart is heavy for the lost. I lift up to You _____.

Please save them in Your great mercy and love. Grant them eternal life, that they may know You, the only true God, and Jesus Christ whom You have sent. For You so love them that You gave Jesus that they might believe and not perish but have eternal life. Oh, Father save them, please!

Prayer for these tumultuous times

Heavenly Father, thank You that You silence the roar of the seas, waves, and the tumult of the nations. Thank You that You are with me, You are my God, You will help and protect Your children. Help me to be strong and courageous, remembering You are with me wherever I go. Thank You that You will not fail me or forsake me.

Thank You, Father that no weapon forged against me will prosper and every tongue that accuses me in judgment, will be condemned. Thank You that You vindicate Your children. Help me to remember not to fear man, but to keep a holy reverence for You. Thank You that Your peace gives me the ability to keep my heart untroubled and without fear.

Father, I lift up my concerns for this troublesome world into Your strong hands so that I may have Your peace which passes understanding.

I ask these things in the name of Your Son, Jesus Christ, who is our Savior. Amen.

Prayer for loved ones

Father God I come to You humbly asking for help for my loved ones. The needs are so great. The problems are so big. Oh, Father thank You that You are bigger than any need or problem. Thank You that You are never boxed in by earthly solutions. You do exceedingly, abundantly more than we can ask or imagine. Nothing is impossible for You.

Father for those who are afraid to give themselves fully to You, I pray that their needs and difficulties will bring them fully to You. Show them Your great love, grace, and mercy. Rock their world to rock them straight to Your loving heart.

Thank You that Your power surpasses every trouble in this world. Hands up, heart open, I ask for Your mighty Red Sea parting deliverance for my friends and loved ones. Open their hearts to experience You. Comfort, heal, show them Your provision, bless them to see You work, to see You, to see Your glory that all may see and worship You!

A prayer against racism

Please Heavenly Father we ask for Your love to wash over our country and world. Oh Father, help us to rise up in love to stop the hate against our brothers and sisters.

Help us to love with Your love. Father, we ask for Your power to defeat the evil, demonic forces of racism. Help us to link hands in prayer, link hands in person, link hands in Your love to stop the hate and violence. Cover my friends with Your protection who are afraid.

We ask for Your unity to flow, Your love to flow, Your healing to flow that we may walk as one. Father, we love You. Bring us together in Your love. Thank You that one day we will all be together "from every nation and all tribes and peoples and tongues" (Revelation 7:9) Oh, what joy when we will all be together!

I ask these things in the name of Your Son, Jesus Christ, who is our Savior. Amen.

Prayer for the restless

Heavenly Father, I am so restless. So very restless. I need You. I am desperate for You. As David cried out to You, I also cry out to You. My soul thirsts for You. My soul longs for You.

Come near Lord, please come near. Reveal any wicked way in me, forgive me, cleanse me, renew me, and restore the joy of my salvation.

I need You. I don't come to You requesting the fulfillment of an earthly need but am seeking a desperate filling of my soul with the presence of You. Because in Your presence, in the light of Your love, everything else fades. And in You, I find all I need, all I want, all I desire.

St. Augustine wrote, "Our Heart is Restless until it rests in You." O Father, I am so very restless, so I come to You. And I come in faith, trusting You, and believing Your word which promises, "those who know Your name will put their trust in You, for You, O Lord, have not forsaken those who seek You." (Psalm 9:10, NASB)

Thank You, Father that You hear our cries, You care, and You love me. I place myself in Your loving hands as you still my restless soul.

I ask these things in the name of Your Son, Jesus Christ, who is my Savior. Amen.

"O God, You are my God; I shall seek You earnestly; my soul thirsts for You, my flesh yearns for You, in a dry and weary land where there is no water. As the deer pants for the water brooks, so my soul pants for You, O God." (Psalm 63:1, Psalm 42:1, NASB)

"To You, O Lord, I lift up my soul." (Psalm 25:1, NASB)

"Seek the Lord while He may be found; call upon Him while He is near." (Isaiah 55:6, NASB)

"Return, O Lord, rescue my soul; save me because of Your lovingkindness." (Psalm 6:4, NASB)

"Hear, O Lord, and be gracious to me; O Lord, be my helper." (Psalm 30:10, NASB)

"Do not call to mind the former things or ponder things of the past. Behold, I will do something new, now it will spring forth; will you not be aware of it? I will even make a roadway in the wilderness, rivers in the desert." (Isaiah 43:18-19, NASB)

"You have turned for me my mourning into dancing; You have loosed my sackcloth and girded me with gladness, that my soul may sing praise to You and not be silent. O Lord my God, I will give thanks to You forever." (Psalm 30:11-12, NASB)

Prayer for when the enemy comes like a flood

If Satan is coming against you like a flood, run to God. Run to His word, for Jesus tells us His truth sets us free. As we read God's word, meditate on His truth, we find answers, strength, wisdom, and the reality of who we are in God and the might of His power that works within us.

The enemy doesn't want you to read the Bible, and he sure doesn't want you speaking God's word. Take God's word, apply it to your life, and speak His truth that sets free.

Whatever battle you personally face, find the word of God to help you get through. God will never leave you or forsake you. In Christ, you are seated in the heavenlies, therefore, you have the power of heaven with you. When Satan came to tempt Jesus, Jesus used the word of God. Scripture has power, use it and let God's power set you free.

Taking scripture, I've compiled a prayer for those in the flood. If you would be willing, read, recite, and pray.

Heavenly Father, the enemy has come against me like a flood. I praise and worship You for You are my strong tower, deliverer, and my rescuer. Thank You that I am always safe in Your hand, for no one can snatch me out of Your hand. You are my rock in the midst of the flood. I resist the devil and cling to You, Father. Show me Your treasures in the darkness.

Help me to rest in Your peace that flows like a river, with Your peace, the peace that passes understanding.

Thank You that You lift up a standard against the enemy. You, Father, draw me out of many waters. You promise to intercede in my time of trouble and distress with the enemy. Thank You, Father. You are my refuge.

Thank You that Your truth, Your word is what sets me free. Thank You that nothing is impossible for You.

Thank You that You have redeemed me, I am Yours. Thank You when I pass through the waters, You will be with me, and when I go through the rivers, they will not overflow me. When I walk through the fires, I won't be scorched or burnt, for You are with me. You are my God, the Holy One of Israel, my Savior.

I put on the full armor of God to stand firm against the schemes of the devil. My struggle isn't against flesh and blood. God, with Your armor I will be able to resist in the evil day and stand firm. I'll stand firm with the belt of truth, the breastplate of righteousness, my feet wear the gospel of peace, and my shield of faith is raised to extinguish all the flaming arrows of the evil one.

With You, I will be as a pillar of iron. Father, I know You cause all things to work together for the good to those who love You and are called according to Your purpose. Thank You. I will be alert, stand firm in the faith and be strong.

I will observe Your commandments, walk in Your ways, hold fast to You, and serve You with all my heart and soul.

Your Words are imbedded and rooted in my soul, and I will hold fast and bear fruit with perseverance.

I will be strong and courageous, not afraid or trembling because You Lord are the One who goes with me. You will not fail or forsake me, and You are with me wherever I go. You are greater than anyone or anything and You help and fight in my battles. Praise You!

Thank You that You hold my hand. You are my hiding place, You preserve me from trouble, and You surround me with songs of deliverance. You are my dwelling place and underneath are Your everlasting arms. You drive out the enemy before you and say, 'Destroy!'. Thank You that no weapon forged against me will prosper and every tongue that accuses me in judgement, You will condemn. Thank You that my vindication is from You.

For by You I run through a troop, by You I leap over a wall. Your way is perfect, Your word is tried and true. You are a shield, I trust and take refuge in You, for You are a rock who hides away the sound and godly. You are my shield and You preserve me. For You love justice and do not forsake Your children.

You watch over all who love You. And because I love you, You will deliver me and set me securely on high because I know Your name.

I will call upon You, and You will answer and be with me in trouble, rescue, and honor me.

You are faithful God, and You will strengthen and protect me from the evil one.

You are my strong tower, and I will run to You and be safe. You are my rock, fortress, and my deliverer in whom I take refuge. You are the shield, power, and stronghold.

I will cast my burden on You because You care for me. You will never allow me to be moved for You are my rock and salvation, my stronghold, I will not be shaken. My strength and refuge are in You.

The flood of great waters will not reach me for You are my hiding place, You preserve me from trouble and surround me with songs of deliverance. Bless You, Lord! You train my hands for war and my fingers for battle. You are my lovingkindness, my fortress, my stronghold, deliverer, shield in whom I take refuge.

Oh Father, stretch forth Your hand from on high and rescue and deliver me out of great waters. You are my stronghold and the rock of my refuge. I will trust in You and not lean on my own understanding. In all my ways, I will acknowledge You for You will make my paths straight.

When I lie down I will not be afraid, my sleep will be sweet. I won't be afraid of the wicked, for You, Lord, are my confidence, and You will keep my foot from being caught. I will never be shaken, I will not fear evil tidings, my heart is steadfast as I trust in You.

Because I trust in You, I will be like a tree planted by the water, extending my roots into Your stream. I will not fear during the heat, I will not be anxious, and as I trust in You my leaves will stay green and always bring forth Your fruit.

As I listen to You, Lord, I live secure and at ease from the dread of evil. For You have put more joy in my heart than any food or drink. In the safety of You, I will lie down and sleep in peace.

I dwell in the shelter of the Most High and, therefore, abide in the shadow of the Almighty. I say to the Lord, 'My refuge and my fortress, my God, in whom I trust!' For it is You who delivers me from the snare of the trapper and from the deadly pestilence. You cover me with Your pinions, and under Your wings I seek refuge; Your faithfulness is a shield and bulwark. I will not be afraid of the terror by night, or of the arrow that flies by day; of the pestilence that stalks in darkness, or of the destruction that lays waste at noon. A thousand may fall at my side and ten thousand at my right hand, but it will not approach me. I will only look on with my eyes and see the recompense of the wicked. For I have made the Lord, my refuge, even the Most High, my dwelling place. No evil will befall me, nor will any plague come near my tent. For You will give Your angels charge concerning me, to guard me in all my ways. They will bear me up in their hands, so that I do not strike my foot against a stone.

I will tread upon the lion and cobra, the young lion and the serpent I will trample down.

Because I have loved You, God, therefore You will deliver me and set me securely on high, because I know Your name. I will call upon You, and You will answer me; You will be with me in trouble; You will rescue me and honor me. With a long life, You will satisfy me and let me see Your salvation.

I lift my eyes to the mountains; from where does my help come from? My help comes from the Lord, who made heaven and earth. Father, You will not allow my foot to slip; You do not slumber nor sleep. You are my keeper; You are the shade on my right hand. The sun will not smite me by day, nor the moon by night. You, Lord, will protect me from all evil; You will keep my soul. You will guard my going out and my coming in from this time forth and forever.

Thank You, Father! I love You!

(2 Chronicles 20:22, John 10:28-30, Luke 6:47-48, James 4:7, Isaiah 45:3, Isaiah 66:12, John 14:27, Isaiah 59:19, 2 Samuel 22:17, Jeremiah 15:11, Psalm 31:4, John 8:32, Luke 1:37, Isaiah 43:1-3, Ephesians 6:11-16, Jeremiah 1:18, Romans 8:28, 1 Corinthians 16:13, Joshua 22:5, Luke 8:15, Deuteronomy 31:6, Joshua 1:9, 2 Chronicles 32:7-8, Psalm 37:23-24, Psalm 32:7, Deuteronomy 33:27, Isaiah 54:17, 2 Samuel 22:30-32, Proverbs 2:7-8, Psalm 37:28, Psalm 145:20, Psalm 91:14-15, 2 Thessalonians 3:3, Proverbs 18:10, Psalm 18:2, Psalm 55:22, Psalm 62:6, Psalm 62:7, Psalm 32:6-7, Psalm 144:1-2, Psalm 144:7, Psalm 94:22, Proverbs 3:5-6, Proverbs 3:24-26, Psalm 112:5-7, Jeremiah 17:7-8, Proverbs 1:33, Psalm 4:7-8, Psalm 91, Psalm 121)

Daniel's Modified Prayer for America

Concerned for his people, Daniel prayed a powerful prayer in Daniel 9. Taking his prayer, I've made some minor modifications to pray for our country.

Father, we humbly come before You and ask for America to turn to You. For the people who are called by Your name to unify in love in Your name, to serve and follow You, to live in Your ways, and be salt and light in this nation and the world. As Daniel prayed, I join in his prayer for Your mercy and help.

I gave my attention to the Lord God to seek Him by prayer and supplications. I prayed to the Lord my God and confessed and said, alas, O Lord, the great and awesome God, who keeps His covenant and lovingkindness for those who love Him and keep His commandments, we have sinned, committed iniquity, acted wickedly and rebelled, even turning aside from Your commandments and ordinances. Moreover, we have not listened to Your servants who spoke in Your name to our leaders, our fathers and all the people of the land.

Righteousness belongs to You, O Lord, but to us open shame, as it is this day—to the people of America, because of their unfaithful deeds which they have committed against You. Open shame belongs to us, O Lord, to our leaders, our politicians, our fathers, because we have sinned against You. To the Lord our God belong compassion and forgiveness, for we have rebelled against Him; nor have we obeyed the voice of the Lord our God, to walk in His teachings which He set before us through His servants and through His Word. Indeed, all America has transgressed Your law and Your commandments and turned aside, not obeying Your voice; so, the country is in upheaval and calamity.

Yet we have not sought the favor of the Lord our God by turning from our iniquity and giving attention to Your truth. Therefore, the Lord has kept the calamity in store and brought it on us; for the Lord our God is righteous with respect to all His deeds which He has done, but we have not obeyed His voice.

And now, O Lord our God, we have sinned, we have been wicked. O Lord, in accordance with all Your righteous acts, let now Your anger and Your wrath turn away from America because of our sins and the iniquities of our fathers. So now, our God, listen to the prayer and supplications of Your servant, and for Your sake, O Lord, let Your face shine on Your desolate sanctuary.

O my God, incline Your ear and hear! Open Your eyes and see our desolations and the country that was founded on Your name; for we are not presenting our supplications before You on account of any merits of our own, but on account of Your great compassion. O Lord, hear! O Lord, forgive! O Lord, listen and take action!

For Your own sake, O my God, do not delay, because this country and Your people are called by Your name.

We ask these things in the name of Your Son, Jesus Christ, who is our Savior. Amen.

Prayer for battling the enemy

Heavenly Father, the battle is raging, and I need Your help. You are mighty and glorious, majestic in power. You have made the heavens and the earth by Your great power and by Your outstretched arm. Nothing is too difficult for You.

Your mercies are new every morning and great is Your faithfulness. You are my strength and my saving defense. Lord God You are all-powerful and completely trustworthy. Save me, O God, by Your name, and vindicate me by Your power.

Hear my voice, O God, in my complaint; preserve my life from the enemy. Rescue me quickly, be my rock of strength and stronghold to save me.

Thank You that Your word promises no weapon forged against me will prosper and every tongue that accuses me in judgement will be condemned for that is the heritage of the servants of the Lord. I will give thanks and praise You, for You rout the enemy.

Help me to stand firm in the full armor of God. For my help comes from You, Who made heaven and earth. I lift up my eyes to You, to You who sit enthroned in heaven. Nothing is impossible for You.

I will hope again in You, I will praise You again for the help of Your presence. For in the day of trouble, You will conceal and hide me in Your secret place. You will lift me high on Your rock. For I hope in You, O Lord; You will answer, O Lord my God.

I will praise You, for You will deliver me from my strong enemy, from those who hate me, who are too mighty for me.

You have set my feet in a large place. You are my help, and in the shadow of Your wings, I sing for joy.

May You hear my prayer in the name of Your Son Jesus Christ who is my Savior. Amen.

Verses for when you are in a battle with the enemy

"Be strong and courageous, do not fear or be dismayed because of the king of Assyria nor because of all the horde that is with him; for the one with us is greater than the one with him. With him is only an arm of flesh, but with us is the Lord our God to help us and to fight our battles..." (2 Chronicles 32:7-8, NASB)

"The steps of a man are established by the Lord, and He delights in his way. When he falls, he will not be hurled headlong, because the Lord is the One who holds his hand." (Psalm 37:23-24, NASB)

"You are my hiding place; You shall preserve me from trouble; You shall surround me with songs of deliverance." (Psalm 32:7, NKJV)

"The eternal God is a dwelling place, and underneath are the everlasting arms; and He drove out the enemy from before you, and said, 'Destroy!'" (Deuteronomy 33:27, NASB)

"For the Lord loves justice and does not forsake His saints; they are preserved forever, but the descendants of the wicked shall be cut off." (Psalm 37:28, NKJV)

"For by You I run through a troop; by my God I leap over a wall. As for God, His way is perfect; the word of the Lord is tried. He is a Shield to all those who trust and take refuge in Him. For who is God but the Lord? And who is a Rock except our God?" (2 Samuel 22:30-32, AMPC)

"No weapon that is formed against you will prosper; and every tongue that accuses you in judgment you will condemn. This is the heritage of the servants of the Lord, and their vindication is from Me, declares the Lord." (Isaiah 54:17, NASB)

"He hides away sound and godly Wisdom and stores it for the righteous (those who are upright and in right standing with Him); He is a shield to those who walk uprightly and in integrity, that He may guard the paths of justice; yes, He preserves the way of His saints." (Proverbs 2:7-8, AMPC)

"The Lord watches over all who love him, but all the wicked he will destroy." (Psalm 145:20, NIV)

"Because he has loved Me, therefore I will deliver him; I will set him securely on high, because he has known My name. He will call upon Me, and I will answer him; I will be with him in trouble; I will rescue him and honor him." (Psalm 91:14-15, NASB)

"...the Lord is faithful, and He will strengthen and protect you from the evil one." (2 Thessalonians 3:3, NASB)

"The name of the Lord is a strong tower; The righteous runs into it and is safe." (Proverbs 18:10, NASB)

"The Lord is my rock and my fortress and my deliverer, My God, my rock, in whom I take refuge; My shield and the horn of my salvation, my stronghold." (Psalm 18:2, NASB)

"Cast your burden on the Lord, and He shall sustain you; He shall never permit the righteous to be moved." (Psalm 55:22, NKJV)

"He only is my rock and my salvation, my stronghold; I shall not be shaken." (Psalm 62:6, NASB)

"On God my salvation and my glory rest; The rock of my strength, my refuge is in God." (Psalm 62:7, NASB)

"Therefore, let everyone who is godly pray to You in a time when You may be found; Surely in a flood of great waters they will not reach him. You are my hiding place; You preserve me from trouble; You surround me with songs of deliverance." (Psalm 32:6-7, NASB)

"Blessed be the Lord, my rock, Who trains my hands for war, and my fingers for battle; my lovingkindness and my fortress, my stronghold and my deliverer, my shield and He in whom I take refuge..." (Psalm 144:1-2, NASB)

"Stretch forth Your hand from on high; rescue me and deliver me out of great waters..." (Psalm 144:7, NASB)

"...the Lord has been my stronghold, and my God the rock of my refuge." (Psalm 94:22, NASB)

"Trust in the Lord with all your heart and do not lean on your own understanding. In all your ways acknowledge Him, and He will make your paths straight." (Proverbs 3:5-6, NASB)

"When you lie down, you will not be afraid; when you lie down, your sleep will be sweet. Do not be afraid of sudden fear nor of the onslaught of the wicked when it comes; for the Lord will be your confidence and will keep your foot from being caught." (Proverbs 3:24-26, NASB)

"It is well with the man who is gracious and lends; He will maintain his cause in judgment. For he will never be shaken; the righteous will be remembered forever. He will not fear evil tidings; his heart is steadfast, trusting in the Lord." (Psalm 112:5-7, NASB)

"Blessed is the man who trusts in the Lord and whose trust is the Lord. For he will be like a tree planted by the water, that extends its roots by a stream and will not fear when the heat comes; but its leaves will be green, and it will not be anxious in a year of drought nor cease to yield fruit." (Jeremiah 17:7-8, NASB)

"But he who listens to me shall live securely and will be at ease from the dread of evil." (Proverbs 1:33, NASB)

"You have put more joy in my heart than they have when their grain and new wine abound. I will both lie down and sleep in peace, for You alone, Lord, make me live in safety." (Psalm 4:7-8, HCSB)

"Your right hand, O Lord, is majestic in power, Your right hand, O Lord, shatters the enemy." (Exodus 15:6, NASB)

"Ah Lord God! Behold, You have made the heavens and the earth by Your great power and by Your outstretched arm! Nothing is too difficult for You." (Jeremiah 32:17, NASB)

"They are new every morning; great is Your faithfulness." (Lamentations 3:23, NASB)

"The Lord is their strength, and He is a saving defense to His anointed." (Psalm 28:8, NASB)

"Lord God All-Powerful, who is like you? Lord, you are powerful and completely trustworthy." (Psalm 89:8, NCV)

"Save me, O God, by Your name, and vindicate me by Your power." (Psalm 54:1, NASB)

"Hear my voice, O God, in my complaint; preserve my life from dread of the enemy." (Psalm 64:1, NASB)

"Incline Your ear to me, rescue me quickly; be to me a rock of strength, a stronghold to save me." (Psalm 31:2, NASB)

"'No weapon that is formed against you will prosper; and every tongue that accuses you in judgment you will condemn. This is the heritage of the servants of the Lord, and their vindication is from Me,' declares the Lord." (Isaiah 54:17, NASB)

"When he had consulted with the people, he appointed those who sang to the Lord and those who praised Him in holy attire, as they went out before the army and said, 'Give thanks to the Lord, for His lovingkindness is everlasting.' When they began singing and praising, the Lord set ambushes against the sons of Ammon, Moab and Mount Seir, who had come against Judah; so they were routed." (2 Chronicles 20:21-22, NASB)

"Therefore, take up the full armor of God, so that you will be able to resist in the evil day, and having done everything, to stand firm. Stand firm therefore, having girded your loins with truth, and having put on the breastplate of righteousness, and having shod your feet with the preparation of the gospel of peace; in addition to all, taking up the shield of faith with which you will be able to extinguish all the flaming arrows of the evil one. And take the helmet of salvation, and the sword of the Spirit, which is the word of God. With all prayer and petition pray at all times in the Spirit, and with this in view, be on the alert with all perseverance and petition for all the saints." (Ephesians 6:13-18 NASB)

"My help comes from the Lord, Who made heaven and earth." (Psalm 121:2, NASB)

"I lift up my eyes to you, to you who sit enthroned in heaven." (Psalm 123:1, NIV)

"Jesus replied, 'What is impossible with man is possible with God.'" (Luke 18:27, NIV)

"Why are you in despair, O my soul? And why have you become disturbed within me? Hope in God, for I shall again praise Him for the help of His presence." (Psalm 42:5, NASB)

"For in the day of trouble He will conceal me in His tabernacle; in the secret place of His tent He will hide me; He will lift me up on a rock." (Psalm 27:5, NASB)

"For I hope in You, O Lord; You will answer, O Lord my God." (Psalm 38:15, NASB)

"He delivered me from my strong enemy, and from those who hated me, for they were too mighty for me." (Psalm 18:17, NASB)

"And You have not given me over into the hand of the enemy; You have set my feet in a large place." (Psalm 31:8, NASB)

"For You have been my help, and in the shadow of Your wings I sing for joy." (Psalm 63:7, NASB)

"I will lift up my eyes to the mountains; from where shall my help come? My help comes from the Lord, Who made heaven and earth. He will not allow your foot to slip; He who keeps you will not slumber. Behold, He who keeps Israel will neither slumber nor sleep. The Lord is your keeper; the Lord is your shade on your right hand. The sun will not smite you by day, nor the moon by night. The Lord will protect you from all evil; He will keep your soul. The Lord will guard your going out and your coming in from this time forth and forever." (Psalm 121, NASB)

"He who dwells in the shelter of the Most High will abide in the shadow of the Almighty. I will say to the Lord, 'My refuge and my fortress, my God, in whom I trust!' For it is He who delivers you from the snare of the trapper and from the deadly pestilence. He will cover you with His pinions, and under His wings you may seek refuge; His faithfulness is a shield and bulwark. You will not be afraid of the terror by night, or of the arrow that flies by day; or the pestilence that stalks in darkness, or of the destruction that lays waste at noon. A thousand may fall at your side and ten thousand at your right hand, but it shall not approach you. You will only look on with your eyes and see the recompense of the wicked. For you have made the Lord, my refuge, even the Most High, your dwelling place. No evil will befall you, nor will any plague come near your tent. For He will give His angels charge concerning you, to guard you in all your ways. They will bear you up in their hands, that you do not strike your foot against a stone. You will tread upon the lion and cobra, The young lion and the serpent you will trample down. 'Because he has loved Me, therefore I will deliver him; I will set him securely on high, because he has known My name. He will call upon Me, and I will answer him; I will be with him in trouble; I will rescue him and honor him. With a long life I will satisfy him and let him see My salvation." (Psalm 91, NASB)

What is deep in your heart? Use God's word to voice your prayer. Keep praying, friends. Keep praying! And, "Do not be anxious about anything, but in every situation, by prayer and petition, with thanksgiving, present your requests to God. And the peace of God, which transcends all understanding, will guard your hearts and your minds in Christ Jesus." (Philippians 4:6-7, NIV)

About the Author

Lisa Buffaloe is a happily married mom, author, and speaker. When she's not writing, she enjoys working in her yard, exploring God's beautiful nature, and taking long walks with her sweet husband.

Lisa loves sharing God's unending love and that through Him we find healing, restoration, renewal, and joy.

Visit Lisa at https://lisabuffaloe.com.

Books by Lisa Buffaloe

(Updated July 2023)

Fiction

The Masterpiece Beneath
Nadia's Hope (Hope and Grace Series, Book 1)
　Prodigal Nights (Hope and Grace Series, 2)
　Writing Her Heart (Hope and Grace Series, 3)
　The Discovery Chapter (Hope and Grace Series, 4)
　Open Lens (Hope and Grace Series, 5)
The Fortune
Grace for the Char-Baked

Non-Fiction

Float by Faith
Heart and Soul Medication
Time with The Timeless One
The Forgotten Resting Place
Present in His Presence
We Were Meant for Paradise
One Lit Step: Devotions for your journey
The Unnamed Devotional
Flying on His Wings
Unfailing Treasures
No Wound Too Deep for The Deep Love of Christ
Living Joyfully Free Devotional, (Volume 1)
Living Joyfully Free Devotional, (Volume 2)

Thank you for reading
We Were Meant For Paradise

Lisa Buffaloe

Bible credits and Bibliography

Because the original text of the Bible was written in Hebrew, Aramaic, and Greek, the original language is rich and full. The various Bible versions I use during writing are to find the one most appropriate showing the beauty and the truth of each scripture.

[i] E. M. Bounds, *E. M. Bounds on Prayer, A 7-in-1 Anthology*, (New Kensington, Pa, Whitaker House, 1997), 44

[ii] Neil T. Anderson, *The Bondage Breaker*, (Eugene, Oregon: Harvest House Publishers, 2000), p 23

[iii] Dallas Willard, *The Divine Conspiracy*, HarperOne, , 1998

[iv] Amy Carmichael, *Candles in the dark*, CLC Publications, Fort Washington, PA, p 54

[v] E. M. Bounds, *E. M. Bounds on Prayer, A 7-in-1 Anthology*, (New Kensington, Pa, Whitaker House, 1997), 12

We Were Meant For Paradise

www.ingramcontent.com/pod-product-compliance
Lightning Source LLC
Chambersburg PA
CBHW060012050426
42448CB00012B/2714